The *Emerging* TEACHER LEADER

Six *Dynamic Practices* to Nurture Professional Growth

Margaret Coughlan

Kathy Perez

Solution Tree | Press

Copyright © 2024 by Solution Tree Press

Materials appearing here are copyrighted. With one exception, all rights are reserved. Readers may reproduce only those pages marked "Reproducible." Otherwise, no part of this book may be reproduced or transmitted in any form or by any means (electronic, photocopying, recording, or otherwise) without prior written permission of the publisher.

555 North Morton Street
Bloomington, IN 47404
800.733.6786 (toll free) / 812.336.7700
FAX: 812.336.7790

email: info@SolutionTree.com
SolutionTree.com

Visit **go.SolutionTree.com/leadership** to download the free reproducibles in this book.

Printed in the United States of America

Library of Congress Cataloging-in-Publication Data

Names: Coughlan, Margaret, author. | Perez, Katherine D., author.

Title: The emerging teacher leader : six dynamic practices to nurture professional growth / Margaret Coughlan, Kathy Perez.

Description: Bloomington, IN : Solution Tree Press, 2024. | Includes bibliographical references and index.

Identifiers: LCCN 2024003791 (print) | LCCN 2024003792 (ebook) | ISBN 9781954631175 (paperback) | ISBN 9781954631182 (ebook)

Subjects: LCSH: Teachers--Professional relationships. | Educational leadership.

Classification: LCC LB1775 .C738 2024 (print) | LCC LB1775 (ebook) | DDC 371.1--dc23/eng/20240226

LC record available at https://lccn.loc.gov/2024003791

LC ebook record available at https://lccn.loc.gov/2024003792

Solution Tree
Jeffrey C. Jones, CEO
Edmund M. Ackerman, President

Solution Tree Press
President and Publisher: Douglas M. Rife
Associate Publishers: Todd Brakke and Kendra Slayton
Editorial Director: Laurel Hecker
Art Director: Rian Anderson
Copy Chief: Jessi Finn
Production Editor: Madonna Evans
Copy Editor: Jessica Starr
Text and Cover Designer: Kelsey Hoover
Acquisitions Editors: Carol Collins and Hilary Goff
Assistant Acquisitions Editor: Elijah Oates
Content Development Specialist: Amy Rubenstein
Associate Editor: Sarah Ludwig
Editorial Assistant: Anne Marie Watkins

Acknowledgments

Teacher leadership is a topic near and dear to our hearts. We are deeply appreciative of the professional educators we have worked with in public and private sectors, where we studied and learned more about teacher leadership. We value the collaboration among educators interested in bettering their craft to support student learning. Our focus is teacher leadership, and our gaze has often turned toward how teacher leadership is enacted, developed, and sustained. To this end, it has been fascinating to see how inquiry, such as action research, can provide an opportunity to seek innovative solutions to pressing classroom and school challenges. We have been fortunate to see such teacher leaders in action. This includes teachers who have taught us about leadership in the classroom and beyond, how relationships built among teachers provide space for conversations and growth opportunities outside the classroom, and how to seek better answers so teaching can be more impactful.

We also learned from teachers participating in a master's-level graduate program at Saint Mary's College of California that focused on developing teacher leadership skills. Kathy Perez and her team developed and created this program to facilitate key skills, such as public speaking, building collaborative conversations, and teacher research to support teacher growth and student success. Program graduates exited as teacher leaders, poised to be agents of change in their school environments. Margaret Coughlan further explored the program's impact in her dissertation and learned that graduates felt an elevated voice and confidence in themselves as teacher leaders. She also learned that the day-to-day practice of teacher leadership can be challenging given various circumstances and that leadership can wax and wane during a teacher's tenure.

Both of us have observed this in our current work. The importance of teacher leadership cannot be overstated, and the energy and commitment of teacher leaders make schools thrive. We feel that supporting and nurturing teacher leadership is ongoing. This book is targeted at these educators; hopefully, it provides a holistic approach with dynamic practices that support a leadership path.

Teacher leadership can be challenging, particularly when relationships, demands on the teaching profession, need of new and current knowledge and technologies, lack of support, or fixed mindsets can't support the tension of challenging questions about instruction and student learning among our important educators—teachers. It's been wonderful to hear teachers' questions and the innovative and creative solutions resulting from such questions, all with the goal of helping students. Teacher leadership is a vital, life-giving force in our educational landscape and all teachers have the potential to be leaders throughout their tenure, the various capacities they work within, and as they tap into their personal purpose for teaching.

We wish to thank Douglas Rife and the team of professionals at Solution Tree for supporting the publication of this important book. In particular, we give a big thank you to our editor Madonna Evans, who has been a pleasure to work with and an invaluable partner. We are grateful to Solution Tree for its support of education.

We would like to thank our husbands—Robert, Kathy's husband, and John, Margaret's husband. They were patient with the countless hours spent researching and writing this manuscript. Additionally, we would like to thank our grown children and grandchildren who have all supported us with affirmations and hugs.

Finally, we are grateful to our readers. We hope that, as agents of change in your schools and districts, your journeys contribute to the ongoing transformation of schools as places of continual learning and growth for all—students and teachers.

Solution Tree Press would like to thank the following reviewers:

Doug Crowley
Assistant Principal
DeForest Area High School
DeForest, Wisconsin

Jenna Fanshier
Principal
Marion Elementary School
Marion, Kansas

Colleen Fleming
Literacy Specialist
Calgary, Alberta, Canada

Nathalie Fournier
French Immersion Teacher
Prairie South School Division
Moose Jaw, Saskatchewan, Canada

Kelly Hilliard
GATE Mathematics Instructor
NBCT AYA Mathematics
Reno, Nevada

Johanna Josaphat
Teacher Leader
Urban Assembly Unison School
Brooklyn, New York

Visit **go.SolutionTree.com/leadership** to download the free reproducibles in this book.

Table of Contents

Reproducibles are in italics.

ABOUT THE AUTHORS xi

INTRODUCTION 1
   About This Book 3
   Who This Book Is For 4

CHAPTER 1
Focus on Your Purpose 5
   Know Why You Teach 6
   Reflect on Your Purpose 9
      The Past 11
      The Present 14
      The Future 17
   Create Your Purpose Story 20
      Write Your Purpose Story 20
      Share Your Purpose Story 22
      Connect to Your Purpose Story 22
   Act, Keep it Real, and Revisit 24
   Conclusion 25

CHAPTER 2
Grow as a Teacher and Leader 27
    Teacher Leadership 30
    Teacher Leader Growth 32
        The Leadership Compass 37
        Continual Reflection for Growth 37
        Ongoing Professional Learning 37
    Teacher Leadership Skills 38
        The Teacher Leader Competencies 41
        The Teacher Leader Model Standards 43
    Leadership in Teaching Careers 47
    Conclusion 50

CHAPTER 3
Effect Change Through Collaboration 51
    Self-Efficacy 54
    Collective Teacher Efficacy 55
    Collaboration 56
    Reflective Practice and Dialogue 59
    Professional Learning 60
        Book Clubs 62
        Mentoring 64
        Action Research 64
        Lesson Study 67
        Collaborative Teams 68
    Conclusion 69
    The Nuts and Bolts of Book Clubs 70
    Reflections for Collaborative Inquiry 72
    Collegial Conversations: A Process for Reflection, Dialogue,
      and Feedback With Peers 74
    My Ongoing Journey as an Agent of Change 75

CHAPTER 4
Build and Sustain Healthy Relationships 79

- Self-Knowledge 81
- Emotional Intelligence 83
  - Listen 85
  - Spend Time Together 87
  - Be Respectful 88
  - Be Present 90
  - Build Trust 91
  - Honor Others' Voices 92
  - Communicate Effectively 92
- Conclusion 93
- *Reflecting on My Reactions* *94*

CHAPTER 5
Take Care of Yourself 95

- Avoiding Overwhelm 96
  - Time 97
  - Balance 97
  - Workload 99
- Supporting Resilience 100
  - Build Self-Esteem 102
  - Improve School Culture 103
- Reducing Stress 105
- Conclusion 108
- *Action Plan for Wellness Worksheet* *109*
- *Wellness Check-In* *113*

CHAPTER 6
Cultivate a Growth Mindset 117

- Understand Growth and Fixed Mindsets 119
  - Teacher Mindset About Student Learning 121

    Teacher Mindset About Teaching 124
    Teacher Mindset About Leadership 126
  Develop a Growth Mindset 129
    Be Curious 131
    Practice Gratitude and Optimism 132
    Persevere with Grit 132
  Conclusion 133

EPILOGUE 135

REFERENCES AND RESOURCES 137

INDEX 157

About the Authors

Margaret Coughlan, EdD, is a classroom teacher, district leader, researcher, and adjunct faculty member at Saint Mary's College of California. Her professional work includes teaching elementary students, teachers, and graduate school master's candidates. Dr. Coughlan has worked extensively with emerging teacher leaders as a research advisor for a graduate teacher leadership program focused on social justice and equity. She is a literacy specialist, new-teacher mentor, and researcher. Dr. Coughlan has presented at the California Educational Research Association annual conferences, Action Research Network of the Americas annual conference, and the Leadership for Social Justice special interest group conference.

Kathy Perez, EdD, is an international consultant, teacher, administrator, and author who has worked with students from preschoolers to university graduates. Dr. Perez is a professor emerita at Saint Mary's College of California. She has extensive teaching experience as a general and special educator, literacy and English as a second language coach, administrator, and curriculum- and staff-development coordinator. Her innovative and interactive workshops are loaded with materials and activities teachers can use and share with others. She provides a lively and informative day of hands-on and minds-on learning.

Dr. Perez has worked extensively with teachers, administrators, and parents throughout the United States, Canada, Europe, Qatar, Brazil, Colombia, the Caribbean, Africa, New Zealand, Australia, Thailand, Hong Kong, and Singapore.

Her best-selling books include *More Than 100 Brain-Friendly Tools and Strategies for Literacy Instruction*; *The Co-Teaching Book of Lists*; *The New Inclusion: Differentiated Strategies to Engage ALL Students* (2013); and *200+ Proven Strategies for Teaching Reading, Grades K–8* (2016). Dr. Perez is the recipient of an International Rotary Fellowship and has been selected for the Reading Hall of Fame because of her commitment and passion for literacy and learning around the world.

To book Margaret Coughlan or Kathy Perez for professional development, contact pd@SolutionTree.com

Introduction

This book is about a unique form of leadership: teacher leadership. *Teacher leadership* is often nonpositional, meaning it's not done as part of an official, recognized position. The authority these teachers hold is dependent on their relationships and their know-how and skill as an educator. More teachers across the globe can be teacher leaders in this nonpositional manner than in positional roles, such as a teacher on special assignment, coach, staff developer, or mentor. If all teachers took up the cloak and habits of teacher leadership, we could have schools that truly grow, thrive, and become learning organizations in the truest sense.

This book is about leadership as a way of acting, learning, and thriving, with the goal of making a difference every day for the students in our schools. You might wonder what's different in this book about teacher leadership. Hasn't it all been covered already? After all, teacher leadership has been part of educational rhetoric since the late 1900s (York-Barr & Duke, 2004). The definition and enactment of teacher leadership have evolved alongside the need for teachers to support school leadership in elevating student learning opportunities. A review of literature on the topic reveals that the call for teacher leadership is more urgent now than ever (Bond, 2021; Buchanan et al., 2023; Lai & Cheung, 2015). Why is this so? Historically, the bureaucratic nature of school leadership has identified teaching and leadership as two different roles within schools. However, teachers are and must be leaders, too, working alongside site and district leadership.

Teacher leaders bring with them a deep understanding of teaching and how schools work. They are the go-to people in schools for many needs and have weathered the many educational reforms that have passed through their districts. Such reforms and the last century's industrial view of education have tightened opportunities for increased teacher leadership in classrooms and meaningful dialogue with other educators about how teaching impacts student learning. This has limited tapping into teachers' valuable knowledge and skills for the betterment of schools. It has left teacher leadership as something that sounds great but is not for all.

Paradigms change, making our world more complex. We need more ideas, talents, creativity, and know-how at the table. Leadership understandings have developed—we know that leadership invites leadership. Teacher leadership works the same way. Our understanding of learning environments and diverse schools makes it necessary to seek solutions that benefit all students. Teacher leaders who work primarily in classrooms are part of the solution; they have the capability, knowledge, and drive to create learning opportunities for students. They share the same vision—to work together to make our schools better.

Schools have shifted to more democratic leadership practices; leadership is flattening due to a more decentralized, distributed approach to school leadership. School hierarchies still exist, but teacher leadership has emerged due to a deeper understanding of the value of collective efficacy that teachers build when they work together to support all students' learning. Gaps are visible as we move our teaching practices closer to supporting student learning targets. Across schools, teachers lead in their classrooms. Although their important work may have increased student learning in siloed environments, sharing these powerful teaching practices and collaborating will greatly benefit the entire school community. Teachers who have worked toward bettering their practice for student learning may not have been empowered to lead others in a collaborative, elbow-to-elbow learning partnership or community or garnered the know-how and experience in enacting teacher leadership outside the classroom.

Leadership is an ongoing endeavor, and the infinite horizon of teacher leadership development is exciting (our excitement and passions fill our cups) and exhausting (when our cup overflows and we forget to nurture ourselves, seek balance and health, and recharge). Teacher leadership is all-encompassing—as teachers, our identity and teaching are intertwined. That is why when we talk about teacher leadership, we don't simply talk about collaborating, learning communities, and increasing teaching proficiency; we also talk about balance, nurturing our own growth, the joy of teaching, and being healthy teachers.

There is space for growth as teacher leaders. We wrote this book to fill that space and to provide tools and practices teachers can employ and reflect on as they develop or improve their teacher leadership practice.

About This Book

In our work with teachers and as teacher leaders ourselves, we have identified six practices that promote and support teachers in their leadership work. We call these *the six dynamic practices of teacher leadership*. This book is unique because it views teacher leadership holistically and each practice is part of the whole picture. This means that there are chapters about teaching and leading, while other chapters attend to the whole leader, including taking care of health and managing stress. These six dynamic practices unfold in the following chapters.

- Chapter 1 explores the first dynamic practice, which is to focus on your purpose as an educator and identify your *why*. This chapter sets you up with a strong rudder to guide your leadership journey. Even if waves crash against you, you will remain on course if you know your why.
- Chapter 2 is about the necessity for continual growth as a teacher and leader. Teacher leadership begins in the classroom, yet a teacher leader's reach is beyond the four walls; teacher leaders strive to enable student success through their leadership interactions with other educators.
- Chapter 3 details how to collaborate with others to effect change and explores ways teachers can exercise leadership through professional development and other opportunities.
- Chapter 4 is about building and sustaining relationships. Relationships are the conduit through which teacher leadership works. The need for developing emotional intelligence is explained, along with helpful practices.
- Chapter 5 explores taking care of ourselves—healthy teacher leaders build healthy schools.
- Chapter 6, the sixth and final dynamic practice, shows why a growth mindset is vital as you work with inherent changes in teaching and sustain that mindset as a teacher leader.

This book also includes reflection opportunities throughout. Some of the chapters contain reproducible tools that can help you consider the concepts further. You are welcome to read the book front to back or to choose your own path—consider where your current need is for reflection and guidance. We hope that this book serves as a handy tool that you can revisit and use to realign your purpose and teacher leadership actions during your tenure as an educator.

Who This Book Is For

This book is for teacher leaders—inside and outside the classroom—and former teacher leaders who now work in other educational roles; it is particularly for those who are agents of change, people who want to transform schools for the better. This book invites you to engage in practices that build your leadership capacity by working among fellow educators who share a vision that our schools can be better for our students, and by taking care of yourself to renew your spirit so you can continue to follow your passion. The message of this book is clear: Be a teacher leader! Develop your skill set, both as a teacher and interpersonally. Don't wait for someone to tap you on the shoulder; your leadership time is now. You have the capacity to make schools places of learning and joy. Leadership calls!

Chapter 1
FOCUS ON YOUR PURPOSE

Every child deserves a champion—an adult who will never give up on them, who understands the power of connection, and insists that they become the best they can possibly be.

—Rita Pierson

hy did you become a teacher? What is your purpose? The first dynamic practice of teacher leaders is to focus on your purpose, to reflect on being a teacher—to know *your* story about why you teach. You and your work as an educator matter (Barrenechea, 2022; Day, Sammons, Stobart, Kington, & Gu, 2007; Gaudreault, Richards, & Woods, 2018; Wilfong, 2021; Wilfong & Donlan, 2021), *and* good teaching matters (Darling-Hammond, 1996; Peklaj, 2015; Podolsky, Kini, & Darling-Hammond, 2019; Stronge, Ward, & Grant, 2011) to every student and to your community.

We begin our dynamic practices of teacher leadership with you, a teacher leader. You may not consider yourself a teacher leader, but as you read this chapter, and the rest of the book, you will see that your teaching and leadership are vital in your school and in the education world. This chapter begins by centering on our *why* and reflecting on how our purpose as teachers drives us to learn more and connect with other educators to become better teachers. Doing reflective work and deeply knowing why we teach can help us understand our purpose and passion, and it can motivate us to ask questions, learn more about teaching, and grow our practice as teacher leaders.

Let's begin the important work of understanding our purpose by tapping into the core reason we teach. Think for a minute, then pick up a pen and write a quick response to the following question.

Why did you become a teacher?

_____
_____
_____
_____
_____

Know Why You Teach

The question—Why teach?—is one that novice teachers ask, and all educators revisit, during their careers. There are many reasons people choose to become teachers (Bergmark, Lundström, Manderstedt, & Palo, 2018; Manuel & Hughes, 2006; Rinke, 2008; See, Munthe, Ross, Hitt, & El Soufi, 2022). For some, it might be because of a role model or mentor who taught them when they were in school. The influence of a good teacher cannot be overstated. Another reason people might choose teaching as a profession is to work with children or young people. Helping students develop and grow as people can be enjoyable and personally fulfilling.

Some teachers find joy in working within specific developmental stages. Others love everything about learning and being in school; teaching is their happy place because they get to share the satisfaction of learning with students. Some people also choose teaching as a career because it allows them to support equitable learning for all, making a difference in students' lives and, by extension, the world. Such teachers want to teach to give students more opportunities and to enhance democracy. Sometimes, people love a subject and want to share the joy of this content area with others, and other times the call to teach is the reason people choose this career. This is the heart of teaching—an inward awareness that they *must* teach because education and learning are of utmost importance.

Teaching can become part of a person's identity. When you first entered teaching, you may have envisioned who you would be as a teacher (Chang-Kredl & Kingsley, 2014; Horvath, Goodell, & Kosteas, 2018), but as you learned and reflected more about teaching, your vision may have been validated or changed (Beauchamp & Thomas, 2010; Olsen, 2008). Teachers' identities invite us to act and to build relationships among students, families, and communities. We connect with other educators who share the same bond. There is an integrity to being a teacher that contributes to making a difference in the world.

Here are a few simple reflections we have heard from teachers in response to the question, Why did you become a teacher?

- "I believe that education is life-changing."
- "I always wanted to teach, and I can't imagine doing anything else."
- "I teach to return the gift that was bestowed on me."
- "I love seeing the light bulbs come on for the kids!"
- "I had teachers who inspired me because they attempted to know me. I will never forget them and how they made me feel."
- "Every day is a chance to make a difference."
- "To change the world, one student at a time."

Sometimes, becoming a teacher seems like a simple, though significant, choice. But understanding the motivation behind such a choice can aid our journeys.

Believing that every student deserves a quality education and that such education can better the world is an example of *altruistic motivation*. These altruistic teachers want to make a difference through their service to others (their students). Sometimes, the passion to teach is viewed as a calling or strong desire to become a teacher. These teachers are often motivated to share a love or knowledge of a particular content area with students so they can benefit from that expertise and possibly expand on what they learn. A teacher's passion for learning and desire to work with students beckons, which is an *intrinsic motivation*. *Extrinsic motivation* to teach includes teaching because of external factors, such as the working conditions, length of work year, salary, or personal status as an educator.

The two most common motivators to choose teaching are altruistic and intrinsic (Bergmark et al., 2018; Heinz, 2015), but extrinsic motivations can come into play as well (Bergmark et al., 2018; Heinz, 2015; Kwok, Rios, & Kwok, 2022; Manuel & Hughes, 2006). Career switchers seeking greater stability and reasonable work hours note extrinsic motivation as the source of their career choice (Kwok et al., 2022) and in non-Western socio-cultural contexts, extrinsic motivation is considered a highly important reason to teach (Heinz, 2015).

Research has identified these three kinds of motivators as viable reasons for going into the teaching profession (Heinz, 2015; Kwok et al., 2022). Professors Manuela Heinz (2015) and Andrew Kwok, Ambyr Rios, and Michelle Kwok (2022) further identify *socialization influences* as an additional motivator. Teachers with this sort of motivation were drawn to the profession because of their experiences with school, from observing respected teachers and family members who taught, or because of teaching opportunities prior to becoming a teacher.

For the most part, veteran teachers report that intrinsic and altruistic motivations and their beliefs about their own professional mastery of teaching keep them in the profession far more than any extrinsic reasons (Chiong, Menzies, & Parameshwaran, 2017). In addition, researchers Charleen Chiong, Loic Menzies, and Meenakshi Parameshwaran (2017) find that extrinsic reasons, such as summer vacation, fit the more pragmatic reasons that long-tenured educators remain in education. Having more than one motivation source can be handy because it allows more landing spots in our educational world and throughout our tenure as educators (Bergmark et al., 2018).

According to author Daniel Pink (2011), people have a driving need to make a difference; our purpose is what motivates us to sustain focus, put in the extra effort, and see things through. In the book *Drive: The Surprising Truth About What Motivates Us*, Pink (2011) explores motivation and discusses how external motivators in work and life are not practical or sustainable ways to meet goals or get things done. Pink suggests that the extrinsic carrot and stick reward paradigm was aligned with the 20th century industrial era view of work and learning. Interestingly, education policies have followed a similar approach while attempting to increase student learning. Carrot and stick extrinsic motivators, such as merit pay and high-stakes testing, have been tried. It was believed that rewards (or lack of rewards) would produce the excellent schools that we all want (Ravitch, 2014).

In her book *Reign of Error: The Hoax of the Privatization Movement and the Danger to America's Public Schools*, education historian Diane Ravitch (2014) suggests that the benefits of merit pay were dubious. All in all, merit pay did not motivate, "rather it caused resentment and dissension among teachers who did not get merit pay" (p. 120). In instances where teachers earned merit pay for extra work, such rewards were downplayed. Research on educator performance incentives validates Ravitch's view that an extrinsic motivator, such as teacher performance pay to increase student achievement, is nonfunctional (Speroni et al., 2020).

However, fair wages are important—to both intrinsically and extrinsically motivated people. A competitive teacher salary is critical in building and sustaining this profession. Research shows teachers entering the profession often demonstrate a caring or service-oriented disposition, and the desire to make money doesn't surface as a key reason to become an educator (Manuel & Hughes, 2006; See et al., 2022). In other words, money is not top of the list. If we pay teachers a decent salary, it might explain why an extrinsically motivated person would choose teaching. On the other hand, fair wages would allow the altruistic and intrinsically motivated person to focus on teaching well without the distraction of trying to make ends meet.

Think about the various motivations—altruistic, intrinsic, and extrinsic motivators, or a social familiarity with education due to all the educators you have known. Do any or several reasons to teach resonate with you? Take a minute and write about the motivations that drew you to the profession.

_____
_____
_____
_____
_____
_____
_____
_____

Reflect on Your Purpose

You will progress through reflective and actionable exercises throughout the chapters in this book. These exercises will guide you in reflecting and then acting on your dynamic practices of teacher leadership. *Reflection*, in simple terms, is the "consideration of some subject matter, idea, or purpose" (Reflection, n.d.). Teaching is not only a technical endeavor; it involves thinking about the learner and how to facilitate learning. It is action oriented, which involves reflection. Deeper levels of reflection develop with practice and experience (Larrivee, 2008; Tay et al., 2023; Williams & Grudnoff, 2011). Teacher reflection is about teacher learning that leads to student learning—the goal of education. Ultimately, our reflections help us understand how our work is aligned (or not) with why we became teachers.

Motivations that are connected to our life's meaning are fueled by deep purpose. Purpose is the driver of all we do; it resonates with our lives and is linked to meaningful action. According to author Richard Jacobs (2017), within each of us is a purpose: "Purpose isn't your job. It's *also* your job. You are not defined by what you do. You are *and* you do" (p. 11). This means that your purpose is not defined by your salary, status, or tenure. Rather, purpose is underlying—it is not bound or defined by the job you have; knowing your purpose is primary to what you do. When you truly know your purpose, it drives who you are, what you do, and how you spend your time. And when your actions are aligned to your purpose, your contributions make a difference. Purpose is unique to each of us. Purpose is a creative vision of our work that, as it is enacted, provides fulfillment and helps us make the world better in the process!

If you want to live a meaningful life, you first need to figure out your purpose. Inspirational speaker Simon Sinek (2011) coined the expression "start with why" to focus people's attention on determining exactly what their purpose is. Sinek suggests that once we know our *why*, we have identified *the* reason that motivates us toward meaningful work and life. When we know our why, our work resonates with purpose and leadership emerges because *what* we do is aligned. To Sinek (2011), "leadership requires two things: a vision of the world that does not yet exist and the ability to communicate it" (p. 228). People who have identified their why and act because of it are inspiring (Sinek, 2011). In fact, this action-driven vision inspires others to do what they do—they follow because the vision resonates with the hearts and minds of others.

Think about yourself as an educator. Knowing that you want to make the world better for students or that you want to share your love of learning sounds wonderful, but it's a little simplistic; it doesn't quite convey your deeper reasoning. Yes, the message expresses a feeling, but we don't have a clear sense of *why* we teach without specifics and clarity. We must rely on our purpose to sustain and direct our actions so that we teach well and make a difference in our students' lives. This wellspring arises from deep reflection and consideration about why we chose (and remain in) education. Teaching is important work and investigating our purpose matters to that work.

The following sections invite you to try several brainstorming activities. They provide reflective questions to elicit memory and feeling responses about your experiences, actions, and identity as a teacher and leader in the past, present, and future stages of your development. These sections lead you to reflect on what you thought about yourself and your work as a teacher, including things that felt aligned and things that did not. According to Sinek (2011), "split happens" (p. 183). He is referring to the split between doing things that resonate with your why and falling out of sync with it; when it becomes what we do, not why we do it. There will be a synthesizing activity following this section that culminates in the creation of your own *purpose story*.

Your purpose story is unique to you and who you are as an educator. It answers the big questions of *why* you teach and *who are you* as a teacher. Knowing your why and being able to articulate it is directly related to your teacher leadership development because an authentic why invites others to listen and follow. Communication is important to leadership; how will you have followers (students, teachers, fellow educators) if you can't articulate your purpose? Clarity about why you teach is hard to discuss, but we can explain it when an event is profound. We gain insight when thinking about needed actions that were taken, what future actions we might take, and how or why we might change as educators in the process. This is about your lived experience as an educator during moments when you were aligned with your purpose and when you may have veered off track (and had important insights).

Your purpose story is a living story because it is not over—you're teaching or active in education, and you will run into "splits" during the nonstop change that is part of working in the field. This story is the personal foundation that you firmly stand on every day as you teach and work with students and families in a community of educators.

The Past

So, how do we more clearly understand our own purpose? One way is to start at the beginning and proceed to where you are as a teacher or teacher leader today. It's a good idea to generate memories about your early career decisions that are linked to specific situations. For example, you may remember that you loved school and wanted to be a teacher since you were five years old. Perhaps you played teacher at home with your sibling in your family's living room as you envisioned being one. There are likely several memories that made you want to teach. Following are some questions to recall your thoughts and experiences.

Purpose Reflection 1

Let's dive into why you decided to become a teacher. You've already named the kinds of motivations you may have had entering the profession, but now it is time to locate the trigger—what was the action or experience you recall? Read the following prompts and then write about it. Remember that when you consider why or why not responses, you are digging deeper into the reflective work that touches your purpose.

- Why did you first consider teaching? Do you remember a situation, feeling, or event? What was it?
- What did you think about teaching and teachers? Do you have fond memories of school or a teacher? Why did you like them? What did you want to emulate?
- What did you like or dislike about school? Why? Was school easy or hard? Why or why not? Why was it important to become a teacher?
- What did you envision about the career and the work when you first began? Who did you imagine yourself being?

List the reasons and events that made you decide to teach. No idea is too small or too trivial!

When embarking on our teaching careers, we likely had nascent thoughts about our teacher identity because we had been students and observed teaching. Our understanding of teaching becomes more complex as we teach, and our reasons to teach may become clearer or more refined. No matter where your work may be, this laser focus on *why* you teach is the driving force in your professional identity as a teacher. It's important to revisit your *why* throughout your teaching path because the complex work of teaching both confirms and challenges our identities as teachers (Day, Kington, Stobart, & Sammons, 2006; Flores & Day, 2006; Keiler, 2018; Suarez & McGrath, 2022).

Understanding ourselves as teachers is more complex than simply having a teacher identity (Beijaard & Meijer, 2017; Buchanan, 2015; Kelchtermans, 2009, Suarez & McGrath, 2022). This self-understanding is not static; it develops and changes in an ongoing *personal interpretive framework*—kind of like a pair of glasses that we tweak or modify through our teaching experiences (Kelchtermans, 2009). This is to say that how we view teaching, act as teachers, and receive others' views of our work can ultimately inform what we think about ourselves as teachers (Kelchtermans, 2009; Keiler, 2018).

Your professional identity guides your presence in schools; it is how you facilitate student learning, it elevates your drive to build student success, and it is a catalyst for engendering joy and curiosity in your students. Our sense of agency is constructed as we grow our teacher identity. Agency and identity create a kind of loop; when teachers' actions are grounded in being "the kind of teacher they want[ed] to be," their professional identity is supported (Buchanan, 2015, p. 714). Professional identity and agency are related—teachers take actions that align with their teacher identity. For example, when a teacher seeks resources to support a reader at risk, they are fulfilling their commitment to be the kind of teacher who acts for student success. Teachers' actions are affiliated with the ways they see themselves. But when demands on a teacher's practice erode their ability to feel like a good teacher, identity shifts and agency diminishes. Who you are as a teacher compels you to act—it contributes to your agency as an educator.

The Present

Teachers develop skills and expertise through their work. Deep understanding of what students need to be successful learners grows; teachers ask questions and seek solutions to reach every student. Is it our approach? Do we need to change our pacing or move toward an inquiry approach in our instruction? Thinking about our present practice as teachers is ongoing; every day, teachers reflect on their work with their students. This reflection opens us up to the harder questions about why we teach and how we view the effects of curricular shifts or reforms on our practice and students.

When we look at 21st century teaching and teacher leadership development, reflection is not a simple endeavor—it's complex (Beauchamp, 2015; Larrivee, 2008; Ostorga, 2006). Reflection is "a deliberate pause to assume an open perspective, to allow for higher-level thinking processes" (York-Barr, Sommers, Ghere, & Montie, 2001, p. 6). This process of reflection is more of a critical reflection, which involves deep thought about our actions (Larrivee, 2008; Tay, et al., 2023; Thompson & Pascal, 2012). It's a mental activity in which we consider our actions and those of others, what happened, and what we think. This kind of reflection takes an open-minded stance, which encompasses being able to step outside of our assumptions and biases. Such reflection "need[s] to be broad and wide in its content, but also deep enough" (Kelchtermans, 2009, p. 269) so we can understand how our knowledge, underlying teaching beliefs, and goals are supported or challenged in the context of our work. Following are some questions to help you reflect.

Purpose Reflection 2

Take a minute to think about when you last created something meaningful in your teaching practice. Think about what motivated you to exert time and effort to build the lesson or project or replan an existing student learning exercise. The following questions can help you think about what inspires you at this point in your career.

- Have you had challenges teaching a student? What was challenging? What was the student conveying to you about their needs? How did it make you grow as a teacher?

- What do you notice about the students in your class who are working hard to "make the mark" but are not quite there yet? How did you help them? What have you tried? How are you connecting with others to better serve your students?

- What do you know now that you didn't know at the beginning of your career? What is important now that was less visible to you in the beginning?

_____

_____

_____

_____

_____

_____

_____

_____

_____

_____

_____

_____

_____

Deep reflection invites us to consider our knowledge of teaching and education and invites other perspectives. We can learn, add to, and develop new habits about teaching and evaluate them alongside our own. Reflecting on our practice and our actions as teacher leaders instills professional confidence, competence, and transformative growth that can help us in the multifaceted work of education (Beauchamp & Thomas, 2010; Bintz & Dillard, 2007; Mezirow, 1991; Tay et al., 2023; Williams & Grudnoff, 2011).

Consider how your purpose has shifted or changed over time. The core reasons you became a teacher may remain the same as when you started, but your lens has broadened. Have you considered identifying more ways to help your students learn about diversity or understand more about our world? Maybe you wish to effect greater social change outside your classroom. Our approaches to teaching grow our ability to convey the content and key concepts. Sometimes, teachers want to try new methods like place-based learning or projects. We open ourselves up to the harder questions regarding why we teach when we reflect on what our students learn, how they can apply it, and how we can help them become critical, lifelong learners. Sometimes, our teaching lens narrows its focus to fine-tune a particular content area that could better suit a diverse group of learners' unique needs. Or maybe it's been a while since you've focused your lens, and you're currently exploring and refocusing on what matters most in your work as an educator.

The more we approach teaching with a reflective stance, the more we become practitioners who are aware of our actions, how actions align with our purpose as educators, and how our view of teaching and education widens. Reflection helps us change, usually for the better.

The Future

A teaching career is unlike others. Some careers are like a ladder and folks proceed higher as they gain experience and develop expertise. Although there is a hierarchical order to running districts and schools, teaching is not like that. It is generally a relatively flat continuum. Some educators move up in positional hierarchy for a variety of reasons; this action may resonate more closely with their *why*.

However, looks can be deceiving—veteran teachers are a powerful force in the educational landscape. A teacher's professional life is a process of growing and changing over time, and with this growth comes knowledge about learning, teaching, and how to work within the structures our schools develop. What teachers envision about themselves and their short- and long-term goals can propel them to seek ways to fulfill their self-view and tap into the inner knowledge that their teaching matters (Chiong et al., 2017; Hammerness, 2008; Rinke, 2008).

Through their work, teachers connect with nearby educators to share practices and learn. Teacher leadership is not contained in a classroom but emerges to help support students, schools, and districts. When this happens, a teacher can align their actions with the bigger why—why is it important to connect, learn, and understand with others so all students learn and your school thrives? Teacher identity becomes more multifaceted because teachers embody their why more closely to who they are developing into as educators. Clarifying what you care deeply about and why sets the course. Envisioning your future self as a teacher and leader allows you to realize your dream to make a difference. Writing your thoughts down in response to the following questions can make them concrete and real.

Purpose Reflection 3

You may feel strongly that you are a great teacher and have high expectations that students will thrive and be successful. But, like all professions, teaching can get dull without nourishment and growth. Or maybe teaching is really challenging right now, and you're feeling disconnected from your purpose. It's not uncommon to lose sight of our purpose in the busyness of life. Think about these questions and write a response to any or all of them.

- Has your growth become misaligned with your *why*? Are you "split" (Sinek, 2011) because of classroom climate, school reforms, and mandates? What is on the horizon to help?

- Is your purpose present in the work you do? Do you convey your purpose so others hear or feel it? Do you feel energy in the things you do? Does this energy relate to your why?

- How has your purpose invited community with other education stakeholders (teachers, leadership, families, and so on) because you share your vision with others? Do you feel that your voice is heard? What are some examples of your vision in action outside your classroom?

- How is your teacher identity changing? Does leadership fit into this? How about your voice as a teacher or educator? Imagine a future *you* as an educator who is working in sync with your purpose. What are you doing and how are you a driving force as a teacher or other stakeholder in education?

Create Your Purpose Story

Now that you have completed the reflections, you have done the important work of considering why you started, where you are today, and what you envision for your future teacher self. These reflections are connected; they are parts of a story—your story. The story is a frame through which you act and envision your future self as a teacher leader engaged in meaningful work, You can now tell your story using your past experiences and current practices as a foundation to reflect on your future vision.

Write Your Purpose Story

You have been on an inquiry quest throughout this chapter, thinking about your past, present, and future *why* you teach. These are a few of your stories that you tell, and there are likely others—anecdotes spring up. It's important to know our stories; they reveal what is important to us and how our experiences shape our understanding about teaching, who we are as educators, and what matters in education. Stories inform our outlook and happiness and help us envision change. In teaching, what we tell ourselves and others about why we teach helps clarify our calling and purpose. Our stories can also convey our values and beliefs about education and ourselves as educators (Clandinin, Downey, & Huber, 2009). Collectively throughout our careers, the stories we tell about becoming a teacher, staying a teacher, and deepening our practice to effect change become our purpose story.

To sustain your passion and joy for teaching requires you to deeply know the stories you will call forth when advocating for students, seeking other ways to reach learners, and working to improve learning opportunities for the students in your school community. These are the stories that push you to be a change agent, as a teacher and leader—a teacher leader.

The following is about unifying these thoughts into one story about where you are now and your vision for the future. As we discussed, stories teachers tell have a way of explaining their reasons for entering or exiting the profession (Olsen, 2008; Schaefer, Downey, & Clandinin, 2014). Storytelling also helps us understand and develop dispositions that support our practice in diversity and equity (Baloche, 2014). Your purpose story includes reflections about why you entered education and the circumstances that encouraged you to teach—what did the situations mean to you? What were you thinking afterward? For example, if you were to say, "I believe education is life-changing," a deeper dive can provide more clarity. What happened that showed you exactly why education is life-changing? Why is that important to you? What does it mean in your work as a teacher?

This next step uses the many stories you've told about teaching and yourself as a teacher in the previous reflections. Why do you teach, what have you learned about yourself and teaching, and how has your purpose made a difference to students? Is your purpose clearer than when you first started teaching? Why or why not? What do you need to do to broaden your ability and influence? You can write a summary, create a list of bullet points, or record your thoughts on a smartphone device. However you choose to memorialize it, this is your purpose story. Your reflections tell one unifying story that embodies who you are as a teacher. It is a snapshot of where you are now and where you want to be.

Share Your Purpose Story

Telling our stories aloud to a partner using an inquiry approach helps us clarify and identify the underlying reasons why teaching matters. This reflective strategy involves selecting a key story from your notes that talks about yourself as a teacher or teaching path. You'll need a partner if possible. If you can't find a partner, try audio recording on your smartphone so that you can be both speaker and listener (although this limits the reflection opportunity). What do these stories mean to you?

In the following activity, detailed in figure 1.1, you will share your stories with a partner. Your partner listens, then tells you what they heard you say about teaching—your views as a teacher and your passion to teach—and asks clarifying questions. Through this process, you will find that you articulate what is important about why you teach through the stories you share.

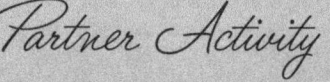

- Partner A tells stories to Partner B about becoming a teacher (this may take about five to eight minutes).
- Partner B paraphrases what they heard Partner A say. *"I heard you say . . ."* Partner B uses the words of Partner A. (Do not put words in their mouth or tell them your opinions about their stories.)
- Partner B asks for clarifying statements about the story, such as:
  - What emotions did you feel at the time or do you feel right now?
  - What is the significance of a specific element of your story?
  - What might you do next or what actions will you take in the future because of this story?

FIGURE 1.1: Purpose story partner sharing activity.

Connect to Your Purpose Story

Imagine that you are going to stand up in front of a video camera and do a TED Talk titled, "I am a teacher because . . ." Or, to get more personal, imagine that you are presenting an inspirational speech titled the same to the families you work with. Remember, this message is important! You have spent time crafting, revising, and practicing it until you have the words exactly right.

Focus on Your Purpose | 23

Now that you've told your story to a partner and reflected about the deeper reason you have this passion to teach well, think about your important stories. What do they mean to you? Why are they important? What do they tell you about education and making a difference? Write your stories down and what they mean. If you'd rather reflect in a graphic, make a detailed web that portrays the story, your key understandings and feelings, and what they mean to you in your teaching life. What emerged from your conversation with your partner about the events you discussed? Was there a theme? What derailed you? What kept you going?

_____
_____
_____
_____
_____
_____
_____
_____
_____
_____
_____
_____
_____
_____
_____
_____
_____
_____
_____
_____
_____
_____

Your presence, memory, and insights from these stories are important because they portray your passions and values in teaching. They highlight what matters most to you as a teacher, and emphasize that you are committed to making a difference in your students' lives, and to making the world better because of what you do—teach.

Now read it. As you read, are you all in? Do you feel your commitment? Have you named your big why? Go back and refine your message if you wish.

Act, Keep it Real, and Revisit

Now that you have written your purpose story, there are several key things to do: act, keep it real, and revisit the purpose story you tell yourself and others.

- **Act:** Make your purpose story visible and public (even if public means that people who are at your desk see it). Write your story on a poster or paper, decorate it, and fancy it up! Post your message in front of you on a wall or desktop, or create a poster or art piece by choosing key words that represent your ideas. Put the message on the front page of your lesson planner. This message is your call for action. Hold on to it. Keep it close. If you truly believe your purpose story, it is *the* North Star that keeps you focused on the importance of what you do and why you do it. Even when directives or mandates, new curriculum, classes, or your work environment are challenging—or when it seems like your practice is going the wrong way—your purpose story is your foundation, keeping you stable through adversity.

- **Keep it real:** Back up your purpose story with data and ah-has. This is important because doing so provides a feedback loop, one that you can reflect on later in the school year. Although we can experience negativity, check in on this kind of feedback—ask why this negativity is jarring to your authentic purpose to teach rather than viewing it as a criticism. Keep the notes that students, parents, colleagues, and leaders write to you that resonate with your why or that help clarify what you need to do. These notes are data-driven, helpful ways to remind you that your work as a passionate educator is evident to others.

  Another feedback source that helps us notice if we are moving from envisioning our purpose story to acting on it are the ah-has that delightfully appear when our class or a student does or says something profound; it means insight and learning has occurred. Keep a reflective journal of these data—if journaling is not your style, use a spot in your lesson plan book to record these nuggets. Give them a big star in your favorite color. Keep them in mind and keep your purpose story alive. This is important when teaching gets tricky.

- **Revisit:** Finally, make a date. We all know that the school year begins with high hopes and joy. It's kind of like New Year's Day. We have an idea of what we want to do this year, we set some professional goals that we want to carry forward from last year, and we thought about how we might put them into practice. However, after a little while, the start of the school year can be a heavy lift. It takes time and energy to organize and plan curriculum, gather the beginning-of-year data, help students grasp the structure of our learning environment, and navigate how to learn in our classrooms. It can be exhausting. Our joy from the start of the school year might take a dip while we balance individual students' learning needs, curriculum, committee work, and the need to teach authentically and creatively while aligning with district goals and standards. It's time to have a date with your purpose story.

Before the school year starts, put a date mid-year on your calendar to review and revisit your story, purpose, and goals. Do you still have the same goals? If not, what has changed? Whatever your students need, revisiting your purpose can provide the necessary jumpstart.

Conclusion

This chapter is about you, your purpose, and what motivates you to teach well. The first dynamic practice of teacher leadership is knowing your purpose, keeping it front and center, and revisiting and clarifying your *why* throughout your educational career. Why you teach is vital to your work and your leadership as a teacher leader. We build our teacher identity through the work we do, reflecting and refining our practice personally and in the company of others, and by learning more about teaching. Your presence, passion, and purpose reach your students and invite them to learn along with you.

Chapter 2

GROW AS A TEACHER AND LEADER

> *If your actions inspire others to dream more, learn more, do more and become more, you are a leader.*
>
> —John Quincy Adams

hat is it about teaching that invites leadership? To put it another way, did you envision yourself as a leader when you became a teacher? Teachers who are grounded in their *why* invite followers (students and other teachers) along with them. This is easy to spot when you see an inspirational teacher (Sammons, Lindorff, Ortega, & Kington, 2016). Inspirational teachers are great teachers. To teach well means that learning is nonstop throughout your career because of your quest to become a better teacher (Steele, 2009). Such teachers are learners; "they wonder, inquire, read, listen, demand, hypothesize, challenge, and question—themselves and others" (Steele, 2009, p. 230).

Teacher learning is important because teaching (and learning) does not exist in a vacuum. The world is in constant change, and a deep understanding of your content area, your students, teaching strategies, and the complex function of education in society are key elements woven into the fabric of your work. Leadership learning is an important component of this too. The second dynamic practice of teacher leadership is to continually grow as a teacher and leader. A teacher's purpose, passion, and conviction to improve learning for students develops and sustains teacher leadership inside and outside the classroom.

Take a moment to consider your definition of leadership, and think about the leaders you know. What makes them leaders? The following questions can help you start thinking more about leadership.

How would you describe a great leader?

_____
_____
_____
_____
_____

What do effective leaders do? (Be specific.)

_____
_____
_____
_____
_____

What leadership is visible in your school?

_____
_____
_____
_____
_____
_____

*D*o you think of yourself as a leader? Why or why not?

_____
_____
_____
_____
_____

*I*s there anything holding you back from leadership?

_____
_____
_____
_____
_____

Leadership is everywhere. It's hard to miss the leadership of a favorite coach, principal, or community leader. A visionary leader has an internal view of what can be. They believe great things can happen when their organization is focused on the mission, what is important, and the heart of why it exists. We can see from these leaders' actions and words that they are focused and driven because this work is meaningful and aligns with their vision of what the team or school can be. They know that what they do and how they act as leaders makes a difference. Remember the *why* we talked about from chapter 1 (page 5; Sinek, 2011)? Leaders are committed to their vision and move toward its enactment. The visionary leader is not satisfied with what has worked in the past but is interested in connecting with others who can move the vision forward. Such a leader is also a learner who seeks new ideas, gathers feedback, listens to others, and has a high degree of reflection about their work and how it impacts others.

In a very broad sense, leadership is a relationship of influence that makes things happen. Author John Maxwell (2007) describes this relationship as his Law of Influence. He suggests that people cannot be leaders without influence. In education, this influence is linked to our know-how and vision about education. Teachers who are committed to making education accessible to all are continual learners and connect with others who share this view to increase their leadership opportunities and practices (Collinson, 2012). Kevin Cashman (2008), a leadership writer and professor who identifies that leaders inspire others by *who they are*, describes leadership as "an authentic relationship of influence that creates value" (p. 24). In essence, this inward-looking view of leadership raises consciousness about how we connect our leadership in education to our purpose, passion, and values. Cashman (2008) believes our inner capabilities have great potential to help our organizations thrive, stating, "The more we can unleash our whole capabilities—mind, body, spirit—the more value we can create within and outside of our organizations" (p. xxxii). Schools need teachers who are leaders.

Teacher Leadership

Teaching creates value in our students' individual and collective growth, contributing to more equitable and democratic societies. Schoolwide leadership is necessary to create pathways and change for equitable and meaningful student learning experiences. Schools need varied routes of leadership for schools to flourish. You are a leader because of who you are and your purpose as a teacher, and your relationship with students influences learning and success in school and beyond.

The term *teacher leader* came into educational rhetoric in the 20th century to describe teachers who led student learning in classrooms, provided schoolwide support, and assumed leadership roles to support teachers through the shifts in educational policy (Huggins, Lesseig, & Rhodes, 2017; Wenner & Campbell, 2017; York-Barr & Duke, 2004). Teacher leaders leverage their teaching know-how and collegial relationships to work alongside district leadership and other teachers to transfer policy into working forms of curriculum, instruction, learning, and assessment. In major United States educational reforms, such as *A Nation at Risk: The Imperative for Educational Reform* (National Commission on Excellence in Education, 1983), No Child Left Behind Act (NCLB, 2002), and Common Core State Standards (National Governors Association & Council of Chief State School Officers, 2010), teacher leaders have been tapped to help lead the way.

Teacher leadership is a powerful means to advance school improvement and build professional practices because expert teachers have the professional knowledge base to develop teacher effectiveness (Fairman & Mackenzie, 2015; Pounder, 2006). Teacher leader positions were created to provide instructional leadership and help improve student learning (Mangin & Stoelinga, 2009; Margolis, 2020; Neumerski, 2013; Smith, Hayes, & Lyons, 2016). The make or break of new mandates, curriculum adoptions, or shifts in instructional design lie within the cultures of schools; teacher leaders, by their very natures, are keen navigators between school culture and school leadership (Silva, Gimbert, & Nolan, 2000).

Education researchers Jennifer York-Barr and Karen Duke (2004) define *teacher leadership* as "the process by which teachers, individually or collectively, influence their colleagues, principals, and other members of school communities to improve teaching and learning practices with the aim of increased student learning and achievement" (pp. 287–288). This definition holds true today. In addition, reviews of teacher leadership identify other actions to include in this definition, such as participating in school improvement efforts, learning in communities of practice, having influence beyond a teacher's classroom, taking initiative, and demonstrating teacher agency (Buchanan et al., 2023; Lai & Cheung, 2015). Teacher leadership, in the simplest sense, has been present for as long as teachers have been teaching.

As educator Charlotte Danielson (2006) states, "Every school and school district is stronger when it cultivates teachers as leaders. . . . They are go-to people; they understand the workings of the institution" (p. 37). As the scope of teacher leadership has widened, the function and roles of teacher leaders have blossomed (Bond, 2021; Neumerski, 2013). However, variances in how teacher leadership is defined, enacted, and supported in schools and the multifaceted nature of teacher leadership continue to make a universal definition unattainable (Wenner & Campbell, 2017).

Conceptualizations of teacher leadership have broadened from leading in *informal roles* as classroom teachers to *formal roles* within districts. Largely, these two views are situated within the debate about whether teacher leadership is a role or a function. A *role* approach is specific and grounded in management and hierarchy, while a *function* approach is loosely framed and suggests that teacher leadership is based on influence and shares the "idea that every teacher should be a leader" (Gordon, 2004, as cited in Margolis, 2020, p. 401). Professor Jason Margolis (2020) suggests that looking at teacher leadership through *semi-formal* roles, as "neither rigid nor chaotic" (formal or informal), can help us create new ideas about leadership and learning (p. 416). It can open up new possibilities!

Using a purely role-bound frame, *classroom teachers* are teacher leaders who develop and continue to work on their teaching practice to lead students in classroom learning. But the notion of being role bound does not serve the leadership capacities of classroom teachers who approach their work with an inquiry-open stance to elevate equity-oriented change in their teaching and across boundaries into other teaching spaces (Buchanan et al., 2023). In other instances, classroom teachers also support student learning in a dual capacity, both inside and outside their classrooms. In teacher leadership terminology, *hybrid teacher leaders* assume identified school leadership roles while remaining in the classroom (Smylie & Denny, 1990; Smylie & Eckert, 2018; Margolis, 2012; Wenner & Campbell, 2017). A few examples of these are mentors and department heads.

In addition, more formalized teacher leadership roles expand responsibility and require teachers to leave their classrooms to lead from the outside. It's not uncommon to see positional teacher leader roles act as structural supports within school hierarchies and facilitate districtwide curriculum goals and boost learning success. For teachers, assuming a formal role provides a new career path—one that taps into their teaching expertise while refreshing and expanding their status as professionals (Bond, 2021).

Teacher leaders work hard to better their own practice, function informally and formally in positional roles outside the classroom, and are driven by their purpose and passion to make a difference in student learning (Angelle & DeHart, 2011; Buchanan et al., 2023; Danielson, 2006; Fairman & McKenzie, 2012; Gordon, Jacobs, Croteau, & Solis, 2021). Teacher leaders can be classroom teachers, but teacher leadership is not classroom-bound, nor is it congruent with siloed teaching; no matter how teacher leadership is enacted, it is collaborative and visible. True teacher leaders are boundary-crossers—between grade-level teachers, administrators, parents, and other educational stakeholders—who seek opportunities to make schools places of thriving and learning.

Teacher Leader Growth

Like other leaders, teachers need opportunities to nurture and own their leadership skills to develop as teacher leaders throughout their careers (Simpson, 2021; Smylie

& Eckert, 2018; Yeager & Callahan, 2016). We might not use the term *leadership* in our teacher education programs and school sites to describe our very own practice of teaching. But by not naming our professional teaching practice as a valuable (and perhaps emerging) form of leadership, we don't recognize leadership as critical to teaching and learning. We also limit our own perceptions and development as leaders. Do you think about how you lead? How often have you heard teachers talk about their own leadership journey as it relates to their professional identity and student growth? When people identify as leaders, they look for opportunities to be leaders and to grow in their leadership development (Sinha & Hanuscin, 2017; Yeager & Callahan, 2016).

Often, important leadership discussions are delegated to coaching, mentoring, school leadership, and administrative positional roles. Making conversations about school leadership overt in teachers' day-to-day work brings them to the table in authentic dialogue and elevates leadership learning as a schoolwide practice. We might know what leadership means because we have a tacit understanding of it. We've seen how it works and have firsthand experience leading and being led. But to know something well is to be able to talk about it, define it, and identify examples of it. We need to be talking about leadership. If we don't identify leadership as integral to our work in the classroom and beyond, we can't begin to understand how our own leadership journey can develop. And we can lose valuable time in creating schools that work well for the betterment of our students, communities, and the teaching profession.

We cannot wait for some undefined future date to develop our own leadership capacity. After all, "organizations that will truly excel in the future will be the organizations that tap people's commitment and capacity to learn at all levels of the organization" (Senge et al., 2000, p. 14). School leaders, including teachers, with a commitment to learning believe that "everyone has the right, responsibility, and capability to be a leader," and "how we define leadership frames how people participate in it" (Lambert, 2003, p. 4). Think about your own definition of a teacher leader and your practice or experiences of teacher leadership. How do you define yourself as a teacher leader? Answer the following questions.

How do you define *teacher leader* and why?

What do you see teacher leaders do? How is teacher leadership visible in your school?

What would help you develop as a teacher leader? Who can you tap into for support?

Grow as a Teacher and Leader | 35

Have you considered setting goals in your leadership development? What steps would you take?

_____
_____
_____
_____
_____
_____

What is your biggest hope as a teacher leader? What is your biggest hurdle?

_____
_____
_____
_____
_____
_____

How do teacher leaders invite others to lead? Why is this important?

_____
_____
_____
_____
_____
_____

Despite the presence and actions of teacher leadership, discussing leadership as part of a teacher's growth and development may be vastly missing from the day-to-day practice of working in schools. Do classroom teachers engage in leadership talk? Do teachers on special assignments or in coaching roles hold such conversations? These are questions to consider while engaging in the second dynamic practice of teacher leadership.

Managerial and leadership work are intertwined throughout teachers' practices. This is not uncommon in leadership—we need managers and leaders to create successful workplaces. In teaching, we conduct simpler management tasks every day, week, and month of a school year, yet we also have leadership actions. Managerially, there are a plethora of tasks to set up and keep a classroom running—creating formative and formal assessments, maintaining student data, and copying or preparing lesson materials. The heavy lift to simply run a classroom often goes unseen by other stakeholders in districts and communities. The teaching part of teaching taps into the passion for student learning, and the managerial part of teaching is more like a job.

It is easy for both facets to blur together or for one stance to unbalance the other, considering the full plates that comprise a teacher's daily life. Teacher leadership, not management, is critical to our work as teachers. Starting with a definition of teacher leadership and continually reflecting on our impact and growth as teacher leaders can further develop our leadership skills.

So, what practices make leadership grow? This is not a new topic to the scene of leadership development (Miller, 2023). The next few sections draw on key elements of leadership development that transcend role. These elements include a vision and mission to make a difference, continual reflection, and ongoing learning. The importance of relationships, self-care, and mindset will be addressed in later chapters.

One key practice is that leaders are driven by their compass—their guide, a point in which their values are connected to their mission to lead. Another key to great leadership is continually reflecting on practice and identifying change to perpetuate growth. A third key element to sustaining leadership growth is continual learning—for teacher leaders, this would be about teaching and about themselves as teacher leaders. After all, "leading is a public expression of learning" (Lambert, Zimmerman, & Gardner, 2016, p. 39). Students benefit from teachers who are continually learning, both within their classrooms and among their peers; they invite learning (and leading) among colleagues.

The Leadership Compass

In business, CEOs often talk about the concept of building a great company. Author Jim Collins's (2001) book *From Good to Great: Why Some Companies Make the Leap . . . and Others Don't* identifies key qualities that leaders demonstrate. One of these is a leader who firmly believes in a personal vision of service to the organization, even over self. Collins (2001) describes this often humble leader as someone who gets things done because of relationships with others and a drive for the organization to improve and thrive. He further stipulates that truly great leaders—those who are aligned in their values and work—make a difference in the companies they lead. These leaders continually reflect on, evaluate, and refine their leadership practice for the success of their companies.

Teachers are leaders in the same sense—we may have roles to fill as teachers, coaches, instructional specialists, grade-level leaders, and so on. However, as discussed in the previous chapter (page 5), teachers have a purpose story—a reason why they teach related to their own teaching story. This is their internal compass. Teachers teach because good teaching matters—it is a future-facing profession. Great teachers have a vision of student learning that they are committed to for various reasons. Because of this vision, teachers learn more, try things out, and seek help from other teachers. Our teacher leadership doesn't just happen or grow because we are in charge of a classroom.

Continual Reflection for Growth

Leadership requires reflection, goal setting, and a burning desire to make a difference. Go back to chapter 1 (page 5) and revisit your purpose story. How does it affirm what you do as a teacher and leader? The practice of daily reflection, something like journaling, is a great way to consider how your compass is aligned with your actions. A leadership habit of teacher leaders is to continually reflect on and recommit to their primary purpose—why every student, every class, every year matters—and noting if what they are doing is aligned with their vision to ensure this habit benefits all students.

Ongoing Professional Learning

Our teaching and teacher leadership practices begin in the classroom. It is in the classroom that we hone our skills to bring content alive and make it accessible for students to devour. As you read this section, you might consider that you already know how to teach, and it isn't really that important to address this topic in a book about teacher leadership. However, teacher leadership begins with deeply learning about and knowing this field and focusing our attention on student learning. Teacher leadership is connected to a teacher's identity—how do we support this emerging identity as a teacher leader?

Teaching is a dynamic practice; it is always evolving, particularly because every class is varied, and student needs beckon us to find ways to help them succeed as learners. This is the joy of teaching! As teachers, we develop our pedagogy—our teaching methods—that we use, such as setting up student-centered learning environments, trying new teaching strategies, or perhaps a workshop approach to teaching mathematics. We work with our ever-deepening content knowledge when delivering instruction. This means that although our districts have adopted districtwide curricula, the drivers of learning are content knowledge and pedagogy. Teachers bring their knowledge of a topic to the curriculum. As they grow and learn, they evaluate their own learning about a topic and create funds of knowledge that are useful in teaching content.

In other words, to teach well is to continually learn as an educator. Content knowledge can grow deep and wide; understanding content in a 360-degree view allows teachers to situate the knowledge in ways to better explain or make it transparent for students.

Teacher Leadership Skills

Teaching and teaching leadership—aren't they the same thing? The skills and know-how to teach well include the following.

- Teaching or facilitating relevant lessons that support learning and collaboration
- Using various types of assessments to validate learning needs and successes
- Ensuring classroom management and environmental supports
- Having a differentiated practice that acknowledges diversity in our classes

Many of these actions are included in United States teaching standards as superb routes to develop and grow professionally, either statewide, such as the California

Standards for the Teaching Profession (Commission on Teacher Credentialing, 2009), or across the United States, the National Board for Professional Teaching Standards (NBPTS, 2024). Through these routes and others, teachers become more proficient at demonstrating the standards in our current practice and through the actions we take toward growth. We participate in teacher leadership when we reflect on and self-evaluate our practice and take steps to grow our professionalism. After all, effective leaders set goals for and monitor their professional growth.

Aren't all teachers leaders? Based on the view that teacher leadership only resides within a classroom, a simple definition could be that teacher leaders are educators who continually strive to be the best teachers for the students they teach. But that is not enough. Long gone is the view that the teacher is the solo pilot teaching in classrooms. We have moved beyond an industrial paradigm of education in which everyone receives the same teaching.

A vision of today's school reflects its diverse community, is inquiry- and equity-driven, and invites student voice and choice into the teaching and learning paradigm (Lai & Cheung, 2015). Schools must elevate competencies of collaboration, creativity, communication, and critical thinking as key practices of student learning (Urbani, Roshandel, Michaels, & Truesdell, 2017). To facilitate these practices, teachers must outwardly connect their students and teaching practices to the larger community of educators—to give knowledge and learn more about teaching. This is like saying, "It takes a village" and making it happen because everyone shares the vision that their school will work for all students to grow together as a solid community of learners. Compare the behaviors of a teacher and a teacher leader in table 2.1 (page 40).

As you read the table, what do you notice about the difference between a teacher and a teacher leader? Do your actions more resemble one over the other? You might be a teacher in one capacity and a teacher leader in another. The teacher leader column is a continuous outward action that benefits all students (not just the ones in your class) and fellow teachers. Teacher leadership includes collaboration and ongoing improvement of your and your colleagues' practices. Challenges are shared overtly because the teacher leader is driven by inquiry. When there is a challenge, teacher leaders are not afraid to learn and seek solutions.

Conversely, a classroom teacher whose immediate focus is on their class and their students' success may be a good teacher, but not a teacher leader. This teacher works in a siloed manner to get through the curriculum and doesn't participate in the strength that a collaborative learning community of teacher leaders has to offer.

Table 2.1: Teacher and Teacher Leader Behaviors

Teacher	Teacher Leader
Knows what best practices are and implements them in teaching practice	Knows best practices and models or shares best practices and resources for bettering teaching practices with colleagues
Self-reflects about teaching and continually works to improve their practice	Works to improve their practice while also supporting the improvement of others' teaching practices
Looks for ways to continually improve	Outwardly models attitudes and behaviors of continual improvement; avoids complacency and works to combat it
Holds professional relationships with peers and school personnel	Holds professional relationships with colleagues and other educational stakeholders; uses active listening and facilitation skills to support communication and learning
Collaborates with grade-level teams, department, and colleagues	Sees collaboration as valuable and encourages and facilitates it
Identifies challenges and solutions to challenges to support students	Identifies challenges and helps provide solutions that promote all stakeholders' best interests
Creates an environment where students are comfortable asking questions and initiating topics	Builds an environment where colleagues are comfortable asking for help, problem solving, bringing up topics that are relevant to student learning, and challenging each other's thinking
Welcomes feedback from colleagues and supervisors	Asks for feedback about performance from supervisors and colleagues

Visit **go.SolutionTree.com/leadership** *for a free reproducible version of this table.*

Although we recognize that teacher leadership begins in the classroom, the emergence of teacher leadership beckons us to encourage change together. We are better together. Keep the preceding chart handy—put it in the front of your lesson planner, post it on the wall to remind you of your leadership path, and continually work to improve.

So, how do we improve our practice as teacher leaders? In addition to bettering your teaching practice per the standards for teaching professionals, teacher leader standards and competencies have been constructed to set goals and identify and acknowledge growth in our teacher leadership praxis. The National Education Association (NEA) published the Teacher Leader Competencies to support teacher leadership development in the Teacher Leadership Institute (NEA, 2018). Also, the

NEA released the Teacher Leader Model Standards as a tool for educators to develop their leadership skills (NEA, 2020). The following sections explore both the competencies and the standards.

The Teacher Leader Competencies

The Teacher Leader Competencies are framed within the practice of teaching and teacher leadership. The foundational competencies are focused on equity, with emphasis on the need for cultural competence and equity work as foundational to teacher leadership and schools. There are five leadership strands: (1) foundational, (2) overarching, (3) instructional, (4) policy, and (5) association (NEA, 2008). There is a corresponding growth continuum for each strand that includes emerging, developing, performing, and transforming. Approaching teacher leader development along a growth continuum sheds light on where a teacher leader might be at different points of leadership competency. It can help teacher leaders see their strengths and where they may seek opportunities for growth. Similarly, leadership itself is a growth-oriented path, and teacher leaders can grow in a variety of ways!

Take a minute to read the following summary of the competencies. As you read, think about your current actions as a teacher and teacher leader (NEA, 2008).

1. **Foundational competencies:** These focus on equity-building practices that promote teacher leaders' abilities to engage with diverse groups and be proactive in creating learning environments that are socially just for all students.
    a. Explore and challenge inequity
    b. Collaborate purposefully
    c. Cultivate socially just learning environments

2. **Overarching competencies:** These focus on skills that a teacher leader employs among all other leadership paths, such as being a good communicator, having interpersonal and personal skills, technological skills, and working with groups with an understanding of how adults learn. Such skill development provides smooth sailing in meaningful interactions among other educators.
    a. Personal effectiveness
    b. Reflective practice
    c. Interpersonal effectiveness

d. Communication
e. Continuing learning and education
f. Group processes
g. Adult learning
h. Technological facility

3. **Instructional competencies:** These focus on going beyond being the best teacher in your classroom. These competencies are based on the vision that sharing your practices outside your classroom and school outwardly benefits all students. This suggests that your work as a teacher leader does not reside in your four walls. It is not enough.

   a. Coaching and mentoring
   b. Facilitating collaborative relationships
   c. Community awareness, engagement, and advocacy

4. **Policy competencies:** These take teacher leadership outside the classroom to serve in other capacities that support schools and student learning. Teacher leaders hold knowledge about teaching that is important to employ as they guide education policy.

   a. Implementation
   b. Advocacy
   c. Policymaking
   d. Policy engagement and relationships
   e. Organizational effectiveness—leading with vision

5. **Associational leadership competencies:** These are about engaging and leading meaningful and powerful collective action to advance instructional policies that impact high-quality teaching. This collective action facilitates policy and practices that are focused on promoting change that supports student learning.

   a. Organizational effectiveness—leading with skill
   b. Organizing and advocacy
   c. Building capacity of others
   d. Learning community and workplace culture

Grow as a Teacher and Leader | 43

What did you think as you read the competencies? Did you notice that the Teacher Leader Competencies are not about being the best teacher in your classroom? They invite you to grow a wider vision in areas outside the comfort of your room by participating with other educators and building collective capacity for all teachers to be leaders in their schools, districts, and beyond. Take a moment to note what you do now as a teacher leader and what you might consider as an area of future growth.

_____

_____

_____

_____

_____

_____

_____

_____

_____

_____

_____

_____

_____

_____

The Teacher Leader Model Standards

The Teacher Leader Model Standards shown in table 2.2 (page 44) identify actions that teacher leaders take as part of their leadership activity (Teacher Leadership Exploratory Consortium, 2011). The Teacher Leader Model Standards provide a sense of how extensive a teacher leader's reach can extend in schools, districts, and communities.

Although they are collectively called *standards*, they are a group of broad *domains*— each domain is an element of teacher leadership. The seven domains are further broken down into *functions*—what teacher leaders can do in that particular domain.

Table 2.2: Teacher Leader Model Standard Domains

Domain I	Fostering a collaborative culture to support educator development and student learning
Domain II	Assessing and using research to improve practice and student learning
Domain III	Promoting professional learning for continuous improvement
Domain IV	Facilitating improvements in instruction and student learning
Domain V	Promoting the use of assessments and data for school and district improvement
Domain VI	Improving outreach and collaboration with families and community
Domain VII	Advocating for student learning and the profession

Source: Teacher Leadership Exploratory Consortium, 2011, p. 9

You can view a breakdown of the specific functions in the Teacher Leader Model Standards (Teacher Leadership Exploratory Consortium, 2011). A look at each domain provides a deep dive into identified actions that can be taken. The domains provide ample entry points in naming or identifying your own teacher leadership development, setting goals, and noting growth. These standards can be used by teachers working in classrooms or teacher leaders in positional roles, such as coach, mentor, or teacher on special assignment.

After looking at the Teacher Leader Competencies and Teacher Leader Model Standards, it is easy to see the potential that a focus on teacher-leader development can have. The competencies and standards can move our vision and practice of teacher leadership outward—outside the classroom and into sharing and encouraging other educators to act on the premise that all students can learn and working together is a best practice. Teacher leadership invites collaboration and conversation. Knowing our paths for teacher leadership helps us set goals and check in on ourselves as leadership learners. Wouldn't it be grand to converse among our peers about what we are working toward in our own leadership? Such conversations are bigger than what we do in our classroom, they are about becoming leaders—our leadership journey.

So, how do we use tools like the standards or competencies to increase our *teacher leadership efficacy*—our deepening awareness that we have the knowledge and ability to be a teacher leader? It comes down to reflecting on your current leadership development using tools like the standards or competencies, lowering your personal walls

Grow as a Teacher and Leader | 45

to let peers or colleagues talk with you about your leadership work and path thus far, and setting personal goals using the tools that align with your work area. Reflection, goal setting, and accountability are key to continuous learning and growth and are ways to increase teacher leadership capacity. Let's try it! Please respond to the following prompts.

*W*hat did you think about teacher leadership before you read the competencies and standards? How did your view of teacher leadership development grow?

___

*W*hat area are you interested in developing as a teacher leader?

___

What walls do you have built around the idea of bringing your leadership practice outside your classroom? How can you get around them?

_____
_____
_____
_____
_____
_____
_____

How can you create opportunities to talk about teacher leadership with other teachers or educators?

_____
_____
_____
_____
_____
_____
_____

What does reflection about your leadership practice look like now? What is a goal you can make about reflecting on your growth as a teacher leader?

_____
_____
_____

Grow as a Teacher and Leader | 47

_____
_____
_____
_____
_____

If we, as teacher leaders, seek development to become more competent, we can become leaders who work among others to transform classrooms and schools.

Leadership in Teaching Careers

Teaching has been described as a flat profession. The egalitarian nature of the job, the equality of pay, and the static position that teachers hold when they teach the same content or grade level for years at a time validate the stability of the teaching profession; it can be viewed as non-growth-oriented. Teaching is a knowledge-based profession, like law or medicine. However, there are "few opportunities for teachers to advance professionally without leaving the classroom" (Berry, Daughtrey, & Wieder, 2010, p. 1). Advancement in the teaching profession often means moving up the hierarchical ladder and leaving teaching behind. This is an interesting thought because advancement is hierarchical to those outside the world of education. The higher you go on the flow chart or the more money you make, the more *advanced* you are in your profession.

Teachers are often in teaching for the long run. When we talk about a teacher's career, sometimes teachers want a different view of education. Rather than look at their work from the classroom outward—from the inside out—they may want to view schools and learning from the outside in. Positional teacher leadership affords this possibility. *Positional teacher leadership* occurs when teachers assume a role in education on a school or district organizational chart other than their current role as solely a classroom teacher. As mentioned earlier in the chapter, positional teacher leadership can be informal (hybrid role) or formal.

One way to change the dimensions of your career path is to try hybrid teacher leadership roles, in which classroom teachers teach while also leading outside the classroom. This could include new-teacher mentors and department heads.

Emerging teacher leaders might also look for more formalized positions. In this case, they would leave their classroom and work full-time supporting the school's or district's needs while working closely with classroom teachers. However, when working outside the classroom as a teacher leader, you must remain aligned with your teacher's compass, maintain relationships with teachers, and build collective learning rather than approaching the position or role as an outsider or administrator. The greatest change will occur among teachers working together as colleagues—elbow to elbow while seeking solutions and improving student learning as team members in learning communities.

Let's take a closer look at some of the ways that teacher leaders enact leadership outside the classroom in formal roles (Harrison & Killion, 2007; Killion & Harrison, 2017).

- **Curriculum specialist:** Some teacher leaders exemplify a keen understanding of content and curriculum standards and understand how elements fit together. Furthermore, they know how to utilize curriculum in instruction and assessment planning as a cyclical, cohesive process. Additionally, curriculum specialists may lead their fellow teachers on standards, assist them in following the curriculum, and develop appropriate pacing guides and formative, shared assessments.

- **Mentor:** Teacher leaders often assume the role of a mentor or guide for novice teachers at their school. This might include doing demonstration lessons, serving as role models, helping novice educators acclimate to the school site and its unique procedures and routines, and dedicating time and expertise to effectively contribute to a new professional's development. The mentor role can encompass many facets beyond curriculum and instruction and share practices and politics as well. The mentor helps their colleagues negotiate the district, school, classroom, and community and grow as a teacher.

- **Instructional specialist:** In this role, the teacher leader helps colleagues implement effective teaching strategies. Maybe a teacher wants to refine their teaching practice and dig deeper into differentiation or become more confident in the use of formative assessment techniques. "Instructional specialists might study research-based classroom strategies" that have proven successful with similar populations (Marzano, Pickering, & Pollock, 2001, as cited in Harrison & Killion, 2007).

- **Classroom supporter:** In this role, the teacher leader primarily works inside their colleagues' classrooms to help them try out new ideas, often by co-teaching or observing and giving feedback. Supporting teachers' collaborative work with peers increased teachers' self-efficacy while reflecting on practice. Improvement through collaboration is an important role for a teacher leader (Blasé & Blasé, 2006, as cited in Harrison & Killion, 2007).
- **Data coach:** Teachers are often inundated with data but lack the skills and knowledge to properly utilize the data to inform instruction. Teacher leaders can open a discussion to engage their peers in sifting through the available data and discuss how its utilization can inform and strengthen instruction. This might include analyzing students' strengths and weaknesses.

In addition to teacher leadership within classrooms, classroom-based teacher leaders might also act in the following informal roles.

- **Resource provider:** Teacher leaders do not hesitate to share their instructional resources with their colleagues. The teacher leader as a resource provider may share website links for further information, articles, books, sample lesson or unit plans, and even formative assessment tools.
- **School leader:** There are multiple ways to manifest their leadership skills, including serving on a curriculum committee, school improvement team, or student study team; acting as a grade-level or department chair; or representing the school on various district task forces or committees. Teacher leaders share their vision of the school and align their own goals with those of the school or district.
- **Catalyst for change:** As an agent of change, teacher leaders are seen as visionaries who are "never content with the status quo but rather always looking for a better way" (Larner, 2004, p. 32, as cited in Harrison & Killion, 2007). These teachers are confident and committed to continual improvement through professional learning communities. Furthermore, they tend to ask questions to analyze student learning and examine ways to improve student achievement.

A teacher leader's work is important and impactful regardless of whether it occurs in a formal or informal role. Teacher leaders can manifest one or more of these roles or actions at any time; in fact, many are fluid and overlapping. Ultimately, it's not about the role. The big questions to all teachers are:

- How do your behaviors and actions embody your leadership?
- Have you thought about your leadership lately?
- What are you doing to better it?

No matter what you do, teacher leadership begets leadership. Teacher leaders invite others to lead. It is a collective endeavor, looking to empower all teachers to lead. We are better together!

Conclusion

Being a teacher leader means that your work (no matter your role) consists of the behaviors and actions you take toward helping students learn and grow. The authority of teacher leadership comes from within—keep an eye on your internal compass, the purpose that beckons you; critically examine your practice for the betterment of student learning; develop knowledge about teaching; and grow in your desire to continue learning. The important thing to remember is that the second dynamic practice—growing as a leader—means that schoolwide, sustainable change occurs from the collective effort of all teacher leaders focused on essential student learning and an ongoing development of teacher leadership practices. Learning more about the multifaceted ways other teachers deepen their own leadership is important to your growth as a teacher leader. Teacher leadership that elevates student learning and builds thriving schools occurs through the collective actions of teacher leaders.

Chapter 3
EFFECT CHANGE THROUGH COLLABORATION

Teachers create and transform energy. They are the dynamos of educational change.

—Andy Hargreaves

o you yearn to move your practice forward and honor your passion to be the best educator you can be? Do you dream of what *can be* at your school with just a few changes to practice?

A teacher leader is an *agent of change*—transforming what is to what *can be*. Teacher leaders are powerful; they are critical to generating and leading change and sustaining the momentum needed for the ongoing teaching and learning that defines great schools. Sometimes, change is a solo endeavor; we can decide to change our diet or set a personal goal to make a lifestyle change, but change is easier and more ongoing when done alongside others. Think about physical exercise goals. When we have a friend or coach who is rooting for us to stay the course, it's easier to make the effort and growth is more sustainable.

When we look at teacher leadership, this unique form of leadership is not a solo endeavor either. Teacher leadership necessitates change *with* other educators. Teacher leadership is both lateral (among colleagues) and vertical (feeding into the hierarchical loop of site or district leadership). The third dynamic practice of teacher leaders is to collaborate with others to effect change that will improve student learning and well-being.

The following are some reflective prompts to begin thinking about yourself as an agent of change.

*D*o your actions align with your passion for teaching? Name an action you took that aligned with your passion.

_____
_____
_____
_____
_____
_____
_____
_____

*D*o you think the collective work of your grade level or team is highly important to student success? What does your collective work look like? What could improve?

_____
_____
_____
_____
_____
_____
_____
_____

*D*o you make connections across your school, district, and beyond to learn more about teaching and how your teaching practices can improve?

_____
_____
_____
_____
_____
_____

*H*ow do you get support when you feel stuck? Where does it come from? Do you encourage the support from others and support colleagues in return?

_____
_____
_____
_____
_____
_____

Teacher leaders transform their classrooms and schools as agents of change. This means that leadership is transformative; teacher leaders seek to transform their schools for the better so all students learn and thrive. This chapter explores how teachers build efficacy in their teaching and teacher leadership practices, particularly through collaborative work with other educators. Such collaboration can bridge the teachers' practice from being primarily classroom-based outward. This is the movement toward leadership that transforms schools.

Self-Efficacy

So how can you, as a teacher leader, move from making a difference in your classroom toward leading in your school and community? It starts with your *self-efficacy*—your belief in your ability to accomplish a given task (Bandura, 1997; Woodcock & Jones, 2020). Self-efficacy reflects your confidence in your ability to do something purposefully and well (Klassen & Tze, 2014). Our confidence, our knowing we are capable, is built from four general types of experiences. Psychologist Albert Bandura (1997) identifies the four ways we build self-efficacy.

- **Mastery experiences:** Mastery experiences occur when we achieve a goal that we set for ourselves. It is the most powerful source that builds efficacy belief. Because of this belief, persistence occurs and obstacles are overcome with effort because the person knows they can succeed and are capable. For teachers, this may be feeling efficacious in teaching because we planned and then taught a great lesson. Another example would be a new teacher completing their first year of teaching.

- **Vicarious experiences:** People also build their efficacy beliefs through vicarious experiences. These experiences occur when you see something modeled and you consider whether it is something you can do or not. When you view the model, it provides a reference from which you measure your perceived ability to do it. Your personal efficacy beliefs can be either high or low compared to the model; subsequently, they will be elevated or diminished by your comparison to the model. For teachers, modeling might occur when we watch someone who we admire teach a lesson and realize the possibility that we can do it too. Modeling also conveys the knowledge and skill in that area. This makes it important that we have proficient teachers modeling instructional moves.

- **Verbal persuasion:** Bandura linked the term *verbal persuasion* with the term *social persuasion*. The efficacy belief is built based on feedback from an important other. In other words, what people think of you affects your efficacy. When you hear that someone believes in your capability to reach task mastery, efficacy is increased. For teachers, we can see this play out in performance reviews or in our daily work; we hear that our work is going well (from principals, parents, or peers) and build positive efficacy beliefs about our teaching. Such encouragement can come from other professionals or from self-talk.

- **Feeling confident:** This falls within the physiological and affective realm. When we are happy and proud of our work or actions, it contributes to a positive efficacy belief about ourselves. Being worried and afraid of success impairs self-efficacy. For teachers, this means that when you feel capable and confident that your teaching has value, efficacy increases.

Given that a teacher's sense of self-efficacy comes from increased knowledge and understanding about teaching and content, when the value of their work is affirmed, self-efficacy further aligns them with their *why*. Professional development fuels our knowledge of teaching, and the dynamics of trial and error (what is often referred to as *action research*) help develop our teaching self-efficacy (Liu & Liao, 2019; Romero-Ariza, Quesada, Abril, & Cobo, 2021).

Collective Teacher Efficacy

When teachers work together, developing teaching skills and increased understanding of what impacts student learning, they can build *collective teacher efficacy*—the belief that teachers working together, monitoring and talking about student learning, can make learning happen for *all* students, not just those in a single classroom (Donohoo, Hattie, & Eells, 2018). Bandura (1997) also identifies collective teacher efficacy in his groundbreaking work, as it emerges from his theory of self-efficacy, except it has a wider swath of impact. Education researcher John Hattie (2023) also finds that collective teacher efficacy extraordinarily affects student achievement.

Collective teacher efficacy means that teachers see all the students at a site as their students, not just the students of any one classroom or grade level. We are collectively responsible for their learning. Education researcher Richard DuFour's (2010) work promoting professional learning communities (PLCs) is based on the premise that highly successful schools work when teachers and other educators learn together and are responsible for the shared success of all students. DuFour talks about collective teacher efficacy and the school as a learning organization.

Hattie (2023) recommends that collective efficacy "is not seen as mere teachers working together and meeting, and the focus of the efficacy needs to be clearly on maximizing the impact on students" (p. 229). Such collective teacher leadership also can systematically eliminate barriers to student learning that have been perceived as insurmountable. This kind of teacher leadership asks us to work beyond ourselves (and beyond the individual classrooms or teams we work in) to connect with and learn along with other educators to make our teaching better for students. It invites teachers to be transformative agents of change! Education leaders Michael Fullan, Joanne Quinn, and Joanne McEachen (2017) note that the leadership that transforms education this century will be "increasingly more likely to come from students and teachers as change agents" (p. 29).

Ultimately, transformation toward collective efficacy *is* the teacher leaders' path—transformation away from schools that function in the 20th century paradigm of the industrial model of education, where learning was designed as a one-size-fits-all model. Transformation to learning models fit for 21st century instruction means that teacher leaders need to connect with other educators to leverage their professional learning by tapping into their practice of reflecting on teaching and student learning. Such work makes teaching practice and teacher learning visible to others as educators collaboratively deepen learning through the whole group's collective understanding and knowledge. These transformative teacher leaders believe in themselves as school leaders, and they work toward developing their own leadership and the co-leadership of other teachers (Pounder, 2006).

Transformation starts with *self-awareness*—reflecting on your actions in and out of the classroom through a new lens. We need to know who we are as teacher leaders and explore our beliefs around power before we can be agents of change while remembering who it is for—our students and communities, and for those who have not benefited or are left out from the one-size-fits-all approach to teaching and learning.

Collaboration

The standards and competencies that were addressed in chapter 2 (page 27) tap into the powerful work of collaboration. In fact, literature abounds with evidence of collaboration as key to the teacher leaders' work (Hickey & Harris, 2005; Woo, LeTendre, Byun, & Schussler, 2022), and thus, collaboration is central to development as teacher leaders engage with colleagues to conduct collaborative inquiry (Cochran-Smith & Lytle, 2009).

Collaboration comes in many forms, but it is most visible when we talk about teachers working together to advance learning and share best practices (Nguyen,

Harris, & Ng, 2020). But what really *is* collaboration? Think about working with others and your views on collaboration. Write your thoughts in the following section.

How do you describe *collaboration*?

_____
_____
_____
_____
_____
_____

Who have you collaborated with in the classroom? What was the purpose?

_____
_____
_____
_____
_____
_____

Did you talk about student learning, student artifacts, or data from a lesson? What did you learn?

_____
_____
_____
_____
_____
_____

What were your next steps or goals at the end of your conversation?

_____
_____
_____
_____
_____
_____
_____

We have a variety of collaborative conversations with colleagues, depending on the circumstances and our relationships with our peers. It could be said that all teachers collaborate several times a day or week. People might say that they collaborate during lunch or a prep period because they are talking about student learning, materials, a funny anecdote, and perhaps problem-solving a challenging behavior or a lesson that didn't quite work. This is informal collaboration and not quite the same conversation that might be held when, for example, looking at graded writing samples or talking about what can be done to help struggling writers.

There are varying ways collaboration is confused with other actions that involve working together in education (Nelson, Deuel, Slavit, & Kennedy, 2010). Two of these actions are known as *collegiality* and *congeniality*. When we are collegial, people share ideas and responsibility for work that is common to practice. When congeniality is the norm, peace, harmony, and happiness among staff are standard practice, differences can challenge the norm, and conversations about change are nonexistent. Collaboration goes out the window, and the status quo is maintained.

A more robust definition of collaboration, as it applies to teacher leaders, requires teachers to have "shared creation of goals along with joint work—the work is organic, and participants have both buy-in and an active voice" (Woo et al., 2022, p. 40). This means that true teacher collaboration brings all teachers to the table and there is a negotiated agenda. There is no singular leader or agenda. School culture can make or break collaboration. Education researcher Hansol Woo and colleagues (2002) suggest that teachers entering the profession have positive collaborative experiences so they can bring these to their future schools.

According to Hattie (2023), building a "shared language about learning and the impact is more critical than a shared way of teaching" (p. 228). Being agents of change includes advocating for students and building capacity for new paradigms of equitable teaching (Von Esch, 2018). The encouragement from and connection with school and district leadership are vital supports for teacher leaders who work during change (Scornavacco, Boardman, & Wang, 2016).

At the individual level, teacher leaders further seek and devour new learning related to students' needs and the curricular demands of their grade levels and content areas. They are curious and avid learners who have burning questions about how to teach more effectively based on educational research and their own growing knowledge (Lukacs & Galluzzo, 2014; van der Heijden, Beijaard, Geldens, & Popeijus, 2018). But they are not solo heroes, and they cannot lead alone. Teacher leaders support and encourage other teachers in their own growth as change makers. At the site and district level, these agents of change work with their peers to problem solve and come up with new ideas. They are innovative. This includes the important (and critical) work of evaluating student growth resulting from teaching practices and working alongside peers to move away from what doesn't work (Meyer & Slater-Brown, 2022).

Reflective Practice and Dialogue

In chapter 1 (page 5), we used reflection to think about and articulate our purpose and passion—the reasons that good teaching matters. When we think about how we teach, how students demonstrate learning because of our teaching, and our assumptions and beliefs about teaching, we demonstrate *reflective practice*.

Reflective practice is a standard practice of educators that supports our learning about teaching. It can be done individually or in group conversations. As teacher leaders, the value of conversations with other teachers *about* teaching cannot be overstated. Such conversations can get to the technical fixes—to tweak a lesson, try a different mentor book, use manipulatives to teach—but deeper conversations among teachers are the ones that will shift our thinking and teaching. These conversations involve deep inquiry and reflection with our peers and are a form of professional learning.

The deep conversations we have are a "collegial dialogue [which] probes more deeply into teaching and learning" (Nelson et al., 2010, p. 175). Eleanor Drago-Severson (2009), a professor and researcher who focuses on adult learning and growth, identifies *dialogue* as distinctly different from *discussion*. Dialogue is "thinking together and looking at some issue together. . . this is different from discussion, which is more about pressing forward with one's own views" (p. 154). Dialogue happens when we ask questions to explore and understand what a person means by what they say. Discussion occurs when a person has made up their mind and is trying to encourage the group to agree with their idea.

According to Drago-Severson (2009), dialogue supports inquiry and our own adult development—it gives space to hear alternative viewpoints and learn from each other. To engage in dialogue is different from having a discussion. In other words, when you are discussing something, you aren't really hearing what the other person is saying. You are approaching the conversation from your viewpoint or paradigm. When we turn and talk about teaching in our staff meetings or in-service, we discuss how we teach, and we share what we do and what we know. These are not the deep conversations we need to have to grow and develop our practice. Being able to recognize these forms of conversation is a way to center our talking. As a teacher leader, we can intentionally ask questions or clarify the point of the conversation to guide each other in how we talk.

Professional Learning

Professional development is valuable and important because new knowledge and methods can enhance a teacher's skill set. Learning about teaching brings a contagious enthusiasm to both teachers and learners because when teachers are excited about what they teach, students get excited too. For example, teachers attending online professional development about phonemic awareness learn cutting-edge research about phonological processing and spelling. This is greeted with enthusiasm by the teachers because they may feel empowered to better support their spellers at risk. Their instruction will have greater clarity and skill and will benefit students; this can increase their efficacy in spelling, and they become excited too!

Professional learning comes in many forms. We have talked about the National Board for Professional Teaching Standards and the NEA's Teacher Leader Competencies and Model Standards in chapter 2 (page 27). These provide the opportunity to set goals for learning and leadership. Professional learning provides new knowledge and skills. Self-selected professional learning is when teachers seek learning opportunities because they align with their goals for learning and leadership. There are many avenues for professional learning. Teachers learn by attending conferences or in-person or online classes, reading books, and working as communities of learners among other professionals.

There are opportunities to learn from membership in online groups. These personal learning networks utilize the internet and social media (Facebook, Instagram, TikTok, and so on) as a learning platform. There, you'll find many ideas that resonate with what you seek to learn. Personal learning networks can support professional learning. Like all professional learning, there is a caveat—does the learning stay within the teacher's practice who engaged in professional learning in a personal learning network, or does it include collaboration and reflective dialogue that builds capacity among people at the school or grade level where the teacher resides? Does such learning grow collective practices (Prenger, Poortman, & Handelzalts, 2021)? The professional learning conducted on-site with fellow teachers is authentic and grounded in their work. It can foster collegial conversations and dialogue about inquiry and learning.

It is not uncommon to attend professional development outside of school (rather than the in-house professional development that results when teachers critically examine student work and plan a course of action). When we attend professional development, we learn about new research that informs practice. Depending on the topic, professional development may be close to our practice or seem like a stretch. Although some professional development settings take the form of sit-and-get sessions that don't actively engage us, the true value of professional learning increases when teachers can talk, share examples and insights, and collectively reflect on what they learned. And the learning may not necessarily transfer to our teaching work without focused, ongoing feedback. Instead, seek to cement the learning from professional development through inquiry, collaboration, trying out new ways of teaching with feedback, and reflection about ongoing learning.

Since teachers returning from professional development can increase their own professional learning, it's fair to ask, "How do they enhance the learning and leadership of other teachers they work with?" To effectively act as agents of change, teacher leaders invite others to build new or improved teaching practices from professional development learning. Teacher leaders share what they learned and ask hard questions about how the new insights and reflections gathered from professional learning might change practice. Such a question may ask teachers to look at evidence from student work and talk about teaching practice, and then make a plan for change. Or perhaps teachers might dive deep into conversation about how instructional practices need to change given new research-based information about how students learn. Education researcher H. R. M. A. van der Heijden and colleagues (2018) say, "teachers as change agents are skilled teachers who have an inner drive to learn and change education, both individually and with their colleagues at school" (p. 348).

The value of professional learning is twofold. First, students benefit when teachers learn. Second, professional learning is connected to teacher leadership when the learning is shared. When teachers do not have the opportunity or inclination to share what was learned and why it was important, siloed teaching remains the status quo in schools and the powerful benefit of professional development diminishes. Teacher leaders, as agents of change, seek to learn more about teaching, apply new methods in their practice, and pursue connections with educators in this endeavor. They evaluate student learning, problem solve with teachers to try a new approach, then revisit their work through feedback. Although there are many possible scenarios of professional learning, the following sections provide a review of a few.

Book Clubs

Book clubs are an approachable and engaging way to participate in professional learning. You might consider starting a book club as a teacher leader action. Being part of a book club might not be a first for you; they are easygoing gatherings and a lot of fun. Books clubs build our professional knowledge and provide a means for deep inquiry about teaching by discussing professional books. They also provide opportunities to engage in group practices, including conversation, planning, and facilitation.

Reliable book club members show up and do the reading ahead of time. Professional book clubs work the same way, but by reading and talking about professional books together, teachers engage in inquiry that builds professional learning (Andrei, Ellerbe, & Cherner, 2015; Blanton, Broemmel, & Rigell, 2020; Reilly, 2008). This kind of inquiry is reflective in nature and facilitates our adult learning when we hear others' perspectives and explore novel ideas.

Key qualities of book clubs support these reflective practices—openness, dialogue, being able to take risks, and collaboration. The openness of books clubs invites folks who are interested; they are not grade, content area, or position specific. Book club membership is voluntary. Book clubs can be among peers, and you might consider inviting coaches or administrators. Reading and talking together as co-learners breaks down silos and hierarchies that might be present in other district contexts. Book clubs promote a community of learners; people connect over the topic and share their experiences and questions related to the book.

The inquiry underlying book clubs allows for a *critical dialogue* about the book's content and how it "connects to instructional practices and how it might influence future instructional decisions" (Drago-Severson, 2009, p. 193). Teachers who share the same mental space in book clubs can build a collective understanding of important but challenging topics. Reflection with others helps extend understanding and may lead to innovative solutions that later show up in teaching practice. The climate of respect and trust in a book club contributes to a safe space for learning. We let ourselves be vulnerable as new learning is shared, and ideas and questions provide fertile ground for reflective dialogue. Book clubs let us take risks as we put our ideas, hopes, and dreams on display for others.

It is in these learning spaces that insights about new or different practices or teaching stances, understandings about access and equity, and our own views about education are articulated and considered by others. Also, when we hear other teachers' views and experiences, there is a likelihood that people in the group will feel comfortable talking and trying new ideas in their practice.

Starting a book club is straightforward. "The Nuts and Bolts of Book Clubs" provides some guidance and is available as a reproducible at the end of the chapter (page 70). The book club needs an organizer or facilitator. This responsibility can be shared among members of the book club or owned by one person—you! Facilitation skills develop with practice, and book clubs provide an opportunity to work on those skills. Continuous refinement of your facilitation skills grows your leadership presence as a teacher leader. The more we engage with our colleagues in professional learning—being mindful of time and the flow, momentum, and depth of the conversation—the more we act as change agents, broadening insight of teaching practices and encouraging teacher growth.

Book clubs are wonderful, but they are not enough to sustain change. We need to apply what we learn from our book clubs to teaching, and then see how students learn. It's valuable to collect and evaluate data about student progress. In essence, a book club can lead to mentoring, action research, lesson study, and collaborative teams; all of which provide frameworks for cycles of ongoing teacher learning through collaborative inquiry.

Mentoring

Mentoring is an example of teacher leadership at the classroom (and district) level that invites educators to act and lead. In mentoring, the relationship is typically between a new teacher and a mentor. This collaborative focus on professional learning through practice develops the skills of both mentor and new teacher. They participate in a *collaborative inquiry*—a form of professional learning that focuses on developing teacher knowledge and practice with the goal of improving student learning (DeLuca et al., 2014). Collaborative inquiry involves two or more people.

Collaborative inquiry includes dialogue about our teaching practices and important questions about student learning. See the end of the chapter (page 72) for a reproducible list of "Reflections for Collaborative Inquiry." Action plans are devised and executed and then reflection connects our practice to new insights about professional learning. The practice is continuous. Collaborative inquiry is vital for the heavy lifting of learning through mentoring.

The mentor and new teacher each learn more about teaching through focus on practice and student learning. The new teacher develops skill and know-how, which enables them to lead students in learning, also developing leadership in the mentor (Gul, Demir, & Criswell, 2019). The mentor conveys the how-tos and whys of expert teaching by unpacking their tacit knowledge to make it visible. The reflection on practice, supportive coaching, and navigation through meaningful conversations lift the mentor's leadership skills. Mentors work on developing leadership-related interpersonal skills, such as establishing and maintaining good work relationships and collegiality.

Teacher identity is closely connected to the ongoing development of our teaching practices, and teacher leadership identity works the same way. Teacher leader identity is connected to the development of others, demonstrating the powerful practices of teaching and helping other teachers in their work. Teacher leadership takes time to develop because it is a "continual process of capacity building," and mentoring is an ideal path for this sort of growth (Gul et al., 2019, p. 225).

Action Research

Action research—the term initially coined by Kurt Lewin (1946)—has been affiliated with inquiry in education since the 20th century. Lewin valued the participation and insights of the people involved as critical to this cyclic process of inquiry targeted at improvement or problem solving (Johnson, 2020; Somekh & Zeichner, 2009). Action research is a mixture of action and knowledge (what we know about teaching and working in education). Because it is localized to the problem solving of the people conducting action research, it is "grounded in the values and culture of its participant-researchers" (Somekh & Zeichner, 2009, p. 6).

Action research is a way teachers engage in professional learning, and it promotes a cycle of inquiry among those seeking to improve their practice. Imagine reading a book about phonics in a book club. An action research inquiry could follow as your grade-level team looks at students' phonics development and asks, "Will working with word ladders help our students develop phonics?" The word research might sound challenging and distant from classroom practice; however, action research is simply applied research—it is used for inquiry and problem solving. It is a kind of research that helps educators improve practice by seeing a problem in specific student learning or schoolwide, figuring out how to solve the problem, trying out the solution, and determining whether the problem is solved by the new solution (Glanz, 2003). Action research is not like basic research that is used to conduct experiments or involves hefty calculations like statistics.

Action research can challenge the status quo. Teachers who conduct action research develop a critical awareness concerning their area of inquiry and, through research on practice, develop agency to enact change in that area, further developing as teacher leaders in the process (Avgitidou, 2020; Benson-O'Connor et al., 2020; Coughlan, 2015). In a review of teacher leadership in professional development schools, professor Jana Hunzicker (2020) states, "Indeed, action research becomes an act of teacher leadership when the research process is led by teachers and/or when the research findings are presented or published so that others may benefit" (p. 3).

Originally, school leaders functioning as leadership practitioners used action research to solve organizational problems, then it moved into the realm of teacher practitioners. Action research can be conducted as a solitary research activity, as in classrooms (Cochran-Smith & Lytle, 2009), collectively with other educators, such as in school-university partnerships and teacher education programs (Benson-O'Connor et al., 2020; Hunzicker, 2020; Smeets & Ponte, 2009), or teacher induction models (Gilles, Davis, & McGlamery, 2009; Smith & Sela, 2005). Solitary teachers working in classrooms conduct action research as inquiry, yet the more teachers work together as they problem solve and come up with solutions, the greater the impact on teacher leadership development.

When teachers conduct action research in affiliation with teacher education programs or school-university partnerships, academic literature is often part of the inquiry process. It builds professional knowledge about an area of inquiry. In schools, although professional learning is inherent to action research, teachers' inquiry is directed on the topic at hand and the process is less complex. This simpler view can be easier for teachers to manage, given the complexities of their day-to-day work (Johannesson, 2022).

However you do action research, holding reflective conversations about the work involved is vital. Conversations at the university level are within the cohort or learning group, and conversations in schools are within the collaborative team or teacher partnerships. Participating as *critical friends* or as a *critical friends group* gives space and practice to deepen reflective conversations (Blake & Gibson, 2021). These conversations involve dialogue about practices and shifts in thinking that might challenge assumptions. Such conversations also allow us to make suggestions in an approachable manner. We can learn to focus our conversations on dialogue rather than discussion by practicing. Professor Tamara Holmlund Nelson and colleagues (2010) agree that using tools for structured conversations can help teachers develop reflective dialogue. A handy tool to build the practice of dialogue and reflection is the "Collegial Conversations: A Process for Reflection, Dialogue, and Feedback With Peers" tool, which can be found at the end of the chapter (page 75).

These are the basic steps in action research based on recommendations by professors Jeffrey Glanz (2003) and Richard Sagor (2000).

1. **Select a focus:** What is it that you want to work on? Is it important?

2. **Clarify theories:** What do you think about this practice? What elements of the practice will help students learn? How can you teach this in other ways? What do you know about this area of teaching? What do you want to learn?

3. **Create a driving question:** Take time to formulate a question that will guide your work. Make sure it is not too simplistic nor too complex.

4. **Collect data from your classroom and student work:** Think about the various data sources available. Make a list. It is good to have more than one data source because multiple sources of data provide different views of student learning. Select the data sources you will use.

5. **Analyze and interpret what the data mean:** Look at the data you collected. What did you learn from it? Were there surprises? What do you wonder about what you see? What else can the data tell you about your teaching or students? What shifted in your thinking about

teaching? What views do you have about teaching this topic that you didn't have before?

6. **Share the results of your data:** Who can you share your results with? How can it impact your work together? What questions arise? What are the next steps?

7. **Act based on your analysis:** What did you learn about the topic and your practice? What did you learn about inquiry? What did you learn about yourself? What do you need to keep, tweak, or discard? Action research is a cyclical process. How can you bring other educators together to help move practice and inquiry forward? Who else might be involved?

Action research is highly beneficial to teacher leaders because it promotes reflection, helps problem solve, aids in continuous improvement, and is action oriented to solve problems. Conducting action research as a teacher practitioner and leader contributes to professional learning through a focus on teaching practices, our actions as teachers, and how these contribute to student learning.

Lesson Study

Lesson study is a teacher-directed professional learning activity that also builds teacher leadership. It originated in Japan during the 20th century as a way for teachers to develop professional practice by applying new learning to lesson design, lesson delivery, and the analysis of student results (Fujii, 2016; Schipper, de Vries, Goei, & van Veen, 2020). The practice of lesson study as a functional and continuous way to increase professional knowledge embedded in teaching practice has led to an increase in teacher leadership across the globe.

In Japan, lesson study can involve whole schools in a yearlong, continuous learning cycle. This cycle consists of four or five processes depending on how the lesson study is focused. For example, a five-step process might consist of (1) setting common goals, (2) collaborative lesson planning, (3) conducting lessons, (4) discussion and analysis of lessons and student learning, and (5) reflection that deepens teacher learning (Fujii, 2016). This reflection moves practice forward because teachers construct and share new learning through professional development. This involves collegial reflection. Teachers learn through the research facet of lesson study—the research part consists of conducting lessons and seeing what happens, then tweaking and trying again. The practice makes teaching visible and creates a safe space to talk about how student learning is affected by lesson design. In the scenario of lesson study, teacher leadership is shared among the teachers in the group. The lesson planning in lesson study includes conversations around the unit standards and objectives. The previously selected research theme is reviewed and clarified. Information about the students and their needs and characteristics is explored.

Overall, the learning plan includes several lessons, and there are explanations about how the lessons are related to previous learning and how they will lead to future learning. Every lesson is constructed and revised by the teachers involved. The lessons in a learning plan demonstrate cohesion; they have a sequential order to support student learning. The lessons are conducted publicly—meaning that it is observed by teachers during the lesson—and videotaped for later reviewing. The collegial conversation about the lesson is important in building knowledge as what went well is acknowledged and questions are asked. Revisions are made and the lesson might be retaught to another group of students or saved for the next session.

Lesson study can be conducted on a smaller scale, among groups of teachers in a school (Stewart & Brendefur, 2005). Critically planning a lesson, being in teachers' classrooms while they teach, and the depth of the conversations surrounding the teaching of a lesson are invaluable to teacher learning. The emphasis on teacher collaboration and learning with and from other teachers invites teachers to take risks in their own work and to be comfortable talking about teaching with other teachers (Schipper et al., 2020). The nature of lesson study is that it is public, not in a silo. Creation of the perfect lesson is not the objective; it is about the process.

Collaborative Teams

Teachers working together in teacher inquiry, ongoing teacher professional learning, and a focus on student learning and achievement are paramount in building teacher collective efficacy. This professional learning that teachers embody is a *collaborative team*—a group of teachers (not a solo teacher or a singular lead teacher) who ask hard questions about practice, gather data about student learning, apply new learning about teaching and instruction, and work collaboratively to better their teaching so more students learn and thrive. Collaborative teams can vary in size, from small grade- or content-level bands to systemwide. As a collaborative team, it is important to establish a worthy goal that can be solved through inquiry and teamwork. Your group might ask, "Why are we here and what do we want to accomplish?" Then, teacher action follows as teachers work together to answer their questions. Such inquiry can bring in new information from other sources, critically examine student learning and teaching practices, and build the leadership capacity of teachers involved.

Teachers in a collaborative team engage in ongoing professional learning throughout their careers. This learning can boost a teachers' understanding of content and provide opportunity for teaching skill development. Whatever the professional learning venue, teacher leaders as agents of change view teacher inquiry as the driver of professional learning. Participation in learning communities, lesson study, and book clubs are a few ways to connect teacher professional learning with bettering schools so that all students learn. Professional learning can build collective teacher leader efficacy because all teachers are on board, sharing a vision to transform teaching for student learning.

Conclusion

As agents of change, teacher leaders flourish and grow when teaching, collaborating, conducting inquiry for improvement, and working alongside other like-minded educators. Think about your work and what you know about being an agent of change. Then, use the "My Ongoing Journey as an Agent of Change" tool at the end of the chapter (page 75) to reflect on your current work as a change agent and your future goals. It is imperative that teacher leadership is visible in schools, is ongoing, and is supported by learning communities that develop practices to positively impact students' growth and opportunity to thrive.

The Nuts and Bolts of Book Clubs

Book clubs can be in person or virtual. Either way, the focus is on learning!

Get members! There are two ways to do this—by content or by self-selection. Also, your approach to book selection can be wide open if the members come up with the book to read, or you might have a general topic already in mind and then the members choose a specific book from that topic area. Either way, your first communication should be clear about your approach.

- *Content group:* Find group members by going to a preexisting group—such as district, grade level, or department. Send the group an email and personally connect. This group may already have a content area they are interested in exploring, particularly if they are a department. Or maybe not! Professional books are also about development, learning styles, and brain development.

- *Self-selected group:* Advertise in the staff room and send an email to faculty! Advertise at your staff meeting! Don't forget to invite coaches, teachers on special assignment, specialists, administrators, and others. The content area for this group may be wider at the onset and if your approach to book selection is wide open, narrow it down with the group.

Set up the planning meeting. This first gathering is to welcome your book club members. Generate energy and enthusiasm about spending time together learning and enjoying each other's company. This is a short, informal, pleasant gathering. Be sure to have food.

- The meeting is also about planning and talking about books. You might have a list of books or internet links to their summaries. Use group facilitation tools to narrow down the general topic as needed, then dive deep into current books that could be interesting.

- Following a discussion, narrow down the book list to the top four books for voting. Either vote at the meeting or send a follow-up email to select the book. For ongoing reflection during the book club, consider making simple journals to hand out or set up a Google Form for folks to copy and record thoughts as they read.

Organize and take off! Communicate by email to confirm book purchase logistics and book club dates. Check in with school leadership; they might purchase the book for group members as it aligns to schoolwide professional learning. Set up a Google Doc to share the book club schedule that includes the chapters to read, topics, and snack sign-up. (If the group wants to bring snacks—no pressure here! Sometimes teachers' days are full!)

- At the first book club gathering, pass out books and simple journals if you wish. Welcome members every time you gather! Check in. Be positive and easygoing. It's OK if all the reading is not done. It's OK if someone is quiet—let them warm up. Sometimes after a day of teaching, teachers need a little quiet. If the book club has met before, review what was talked about last time and the current book chapters and topic.

- At the start, review the chapters and topic. Keep the conversations going! Plan how you might ask folks to talk (elbow partners, move to parts of the room, or by topic). Ask if others have similar or different experiences, how their thinking may have shifted or stayed the same while reading, or if some part of the reading connects to their practice or to something they have observed or felt. Group size matters—if the group is too big, move people into clusters. If the same people keep working together, try to change partners by doing something as simple as suggesting that folks get up and arrange themselves by birthday months and so on. Facilitation of group process helps things run smoothly.

- At the end of the meeting, hand out sticky notes and have members write phrases. They can either share their thinking aloud or post their sticky notes on the door on their way out. If they post it on the door, add the reflections to the shared Google Doc for all to see. Remind group members about the next gathering and topic.

The following are some prompts you can use in a book club.

- *I used to think . . . but now, I think . . .*

- *I'm going to try . . . in my class before we meet next time.*

- *I appreciated hearing . . .*

- *I have questions about . . .*

Reflections for Collaborative Inquiry

You can use these prompts to develop a collaborative dialogue with a colleague or group.

Instruction

- What are your main learning targets?
- How could you teach the content differently?
- What are the implications for student mastery and understanding?

Products of Learning

- How will students show what they know?
- What are other ways for students to demonstrate understanding?

Examining Student Work

- What will content mastery look like?
- How will students demonstrate their understanding?
- Are there additional ways to demonstrate learning?

Connecting Student Work to Content Taught

- What connects student products to lesson content?
- What are some other ways you could teach this lesson?
- Do you want to modify the content in any way?
- Do you want to modify the student product in any way?

Assessing Learning

- Are there any gaps that students have demonstrated in their understanding of the lesson?
- What more do you need to know about the students' mastery of the lesson?
- How student-centered is the assessment that you used?
- What are some other learning assessment techniques you could use?

Reflections on Collaboration

- How did this collegial conversation improve the lesson?
- Do you have a new understanding of students' thinking?
- What are your next steps?
- What do you need to learn more about?

Source: Adapted from Nelson, T. H., Deuel, A., Slavit, D., & Kennedy, A. (2010). Leading deep conversations in collaborative inquiry groups. The Clearing House, 83*(5), 175–179.*

Collegial Conversations: A Process for Reflection, Dialogue, and Feedback With Peers

Teaching can be a lonely profession unless we build in time to reflect and connect with colleagues in collaborative conversations. As teacher leaders, it is important to develop these collegial relationships that encourage reflective practices and to solicit and provide feedback that promotes reflective learning.

- Assembling a group of colleagues is the first step in this process. Roles should be defined, including the role of facilitator (timekeeper) and the presenter—who has an issue or a lesson to discuss. The rest of the group members serve as discussants—those providing supportive feedback with ideas and suggestions.

- The person who shares the issue should provide as many details as possible, including the context.

- The group then has an opportunity to respond, ask questions, and provide feedback.

- The presenter can respond to group feedback before the facilitator summarizes and closes the discussion.

- This process can be modified and is flexible to meet the group's needs. It should be stressed that conversations are confidential and designed to support each other, not undermine professional effectiveness.

Source: Adapted from Bambino, D. (2002). Critical friends. Educational Leadership, 59(6), 25–27.
Blake, J., & Gibson, A. (2021). Critical friends group protocols deepen conversations in collaborative action research projects. Educational Action Research, 29(1), 133–148.
Chiappetta, E. (2023, February 1). A protocol for teacher-focused PD. Accessed at www.edutopia.org/article/critical-friends-group-protocol-pd/ on October 27, 2023.
University of Illinois Urbana-Champaign. (n.d.). Annenburg Institutes Critical Friends Summary. Accessed at https://ws.engr.illinois.edu/sitemanager/getfile.asp?id=4190 on January 7, 2024.

My Ongoing Journey as an Agent of Change

Teacher leaders are agents of change! They are action oriented.

Think about your teacher-leader path. Where are you? Where are you headed? Use the topics to self-reflect and to set goals. Revisit this to review goals and check on your progress.

Knowledge Builder

Think about your professional learning. What have you done to increase your professional learning lately? Has it been a while since you read a professional book or article, taken a class, or conducted action research?

_____
_____
_____
_____
_____

What have you done to share and build knowledge? How have you invited others to build professional knowledge with you?

_____
_____
_____
_____
_____

My Knowledge Builder Goals:

_____
_____
_____
_____
_____
_____

Student Advocate

Think about what you have done to advocate for students. How have you connected to families? What have you learned about how we learn?

_____
_____
_____
_____
_____
_____

What have you done to promote equity and access? How have you contributed to building capacity for equity work in your classroom or school?

_____
_____
_____
_____
_____
_____

My Student Advocate Goals:

_____
_____
_____
_____
_____
_____

Community Supporter

Think about how you have helped on curricular committees, site committees, departments, and in school functions. What have you done to support the learning at your site? How does this support align with your purpose as a teacher leader?

_____
_____
_____
_____
_____
_____

My Community Supporter Goals:

_____
_____
_____
_____
_____
_____

Self-Reflection and Growth

Think about your work as an agent of change. How is your work aligned with your purpose and passion to teach? How have you promoted self-care toward yourself and others?

_____
_____
_____
_____
_____
_____

How have you demonstrated empathy for others as they work to better their practices and professional learning? How have you invited them into teacher leadership? What actions have you taken to develop relationships?

_____
_____
_____
_____
_____
_____

Self-Reflection and Growth Goals:

_____
_____
_____
_____
_____

Chapter 4
BUILD AND SUSTAIN HEALTHY RELATIONSHIPS

Relationships are all there is. Everything in the universe only exists because it is in relationship to everything else. Nothing exists in isolation. We have to stop pretending we are individuals that can go it alone.

—Margaret Wheatley

Teacher leadership is relational because leadership works through relationships. A teacher leader's practice is situated within the social, cultural, and political spheres of the educational world. Creating and nurturing these relationships allow teacher leadership to happen. Relationships are *key*—to everything. Educator and author Margaret Wheatley (2006b) acknowledges that teachers form these relationships as they engage in their common work—teaching. Leading through teacher-to-teacher relationships is critical for teacher leaders. Such self-created networks have knowledge-building capacity. These networks exist because of the relationships between staff; within them, there is trust.

It is important to grow and nurture relationships. As Wheatley (2006b) states, "if we're to evoke kindness, intelligence, accountability and learning in our organizations, we need to promote healthy relationships" (p. 2). This chapter focuses on those relationships. They are the medium through which teacher leadership functions. Sometimes, relationships can limit teacher leadership and other times they can support the ways teacher leaders facilitate growth (Mangin, 2010; Mangin & Stoelinga, 2011; Margolis 2012; Weiner, 2011).

A teacher leader's access point is in building and sustaining healthy relationships—the fourth dynamic practice of teacher leadership. The connections we have within our schools and communities make way for growth and are a vital resource for teacher leaders (Fairman & McKenzie, 2015). Our own growth as educators, and that of our colleagues and peers, hinges on our ability to be mindful of our relationships, to be present and listen, to communicate clearly, and to share our enthusiasm for teaching and personal growth.

As mentioned in chapter 2 (page 27), teaching has been described as a flat profession—most teachers do not enter the hierarchical ladder of district leadership. Teachers' rise on the pay scale is often dependent on tenure and the contracted step and ladder. Some might assume that a more tenured teacher has more teaching clout and professional expertise, but this is not necessarily so. For these reasons, teaching can become static. Teachers develop their expertise and practice when they continue to learn, reflect on how their teaching impacts students, and work through inquiry to teach better. The most efficient form of such learning is when teachers work with other teachers in true collaboration rather than in silos. True collaboration requires healthy, meaningful relationships.

Other than the identified, more formalized teacher leadership roles we discussed in chapter 2 (page 27), most teachers work within their grade or content area for a significant time—some teachers for the duration of their teaching career. The effort of building, maintaining, and nurturing relationships is ongoing and paramount for teacher leaders at the classroom level because change occurs here. It is here that a teacher leader's relationship with colleagues can break down walls of resistance due to the discomfort colleagues may have about a shift in practice or change of perspective about long-standing habits.

It's a question of relationships; change beckoned by teacher leadership (which relies on relationships to enact such change) is in tension with a teacher's relationship to feeling success in their work (and trusting that this change is worth it). It is also where challenges, due to some nascent working relationships among teacher practitioners, can limit growth (Barth, 2006; Weiner, 2011). In this scenario, the ultimate power of relationships is not readily available, and change is difficult. Here is where collegiality—a shared responsibility for our collective effort—comes into play. When we look at relationship-building actions, promoting collegiality and collegial dialogue makes a difference (Barth, 2006; Nelson et al., 2010). Planned district initiatives and hopes for professional development improvement can become reality when teachers acknowledge that their relationships are precious to their growth. The presence of positive relationships is integral to collegial conversations that help transfer new insights, practices, and mindsets into teaching practice.

Teacher leaders in formalized leadership roles also rely on leveraging relationships to facilitate the transfer of new learning to improve or change existing teaching practices (Mangin, 2010). But formal relationships have an additional element. The difference is in the powerful relationship between teachers who have positional authority (whether district leadership granted it or not) and the informal leadership of classroom teachers themselves. Teacher leaders in positional roles may have responsibilities and accountability to ensure their positional authority is functional, which affects relationships with teachers. Teacher leaders in formalized positions that downplay their authority have greater access to leadership work among teachers (Firestone & Martinez, 2007; Margolis, 2012; Weiner, 2011). For formal teacher leadership to work, classroom teachers themselves must first legitimize the teacher leader's role with an informal, and sometimes critical, evaluation about the capabilities and knowledge the teacher leader really holds in the academic area (Katzenmeyer & Moller, 2009; Mangin, 2005). This legitimacy occurs when formal teacher leaders and their constituents (teachers) tap into their connectedness through their relationships.

Teacher leaders, no matter who they are, cannot lead alone. Teacher leaders also need their principal's support for real change to occur (Meyer & Slater-Brown, 2022; Tschannen-Moran, 2009). Teacher leaders may help move teaching practice forward, but change is hard to sustain without the support of and relationships with district leadership (Tschannen-Moran, 2009).

How do we learn to make this vital element of our leadership stronger? Where do we start? We can't make a difference in our schools if we don't know where we are coming from, so start with some self-analysis.

Self-Knowledge

All relationships begin with who we are because we project our inner self outward, and it impacts how we interact with others (no matter how much we might think we're good at hiding our inner selves). When the workload is heavy or change is complex, we need to understand who we are and what we believe about ourselves as teacher leaders because this is demonstrated as actions. That is why it is handy to start at the beginning—with *you*.

We worked on our purpose story in chapter 1 (page 5), so now let's think more generally about who you are, as a person. If you could describe yourself, you might say, "I am a seventh-grade mathematics teacher, and I've been teaching for nine years." But outside of being a teacher, what else would you say?

Think of all the great things you know about yourself. Are you creative? Artistic? Analytical? These are the things that you bring to the table when you work with people. It feels good when you are doing work that aligns with who you perceive yourself to be. The following questions can help you consider your identity more.

How do you act around people versus when you're alone?

_____
_____
_____
_____
_____

What makes you happy, and what makes you feel valued, and why?

_____
_____
_____
_____
_____

What makes you confident, and what makes you feel unsure, and why?

_____
_____

There are many tools on the internet, such as 16 Personalities (www.16personalities.com) and Truity's Enneagram Personality Test (www.truity.com/test/enneagram-personality-test), that can help you learn more about yourself. But in the end, self-reflection as a leadership habit is a powerful way to understand how we act in situations and how we can improve and grow. In the process, you may also learn that sometimes our approach toward others may not be interpreted as we intended because we all have areas of weakness, things that we don't quite see about ourselves but are apparent to others. After all, our actions can promote positive relationships or they can harm them.

Understanding how we might approach problem solving compared to someone else is helpful in relationship work. Knowing such information can make us self-aware. For example, if your inclination is to approach problem solving from an analytical stance and you are quick to make decisions, this may affect the relationships with others who might approach decision making by looking at all the options and the details within. Knowing ourselves lets us put a hold on an immediate reaction and invite others into decision making. We might frame situations based on what is comfortable, but it might be more productive to push the pause button and think about how others might respond. Please see the "Reflecting on My Reactions" reproducible tool at the end of the chapter (page 94).

Emotional Intelligence

People are emotional and social beings. Although we speak, talk, run, and play in relationships, everything we do is connected to what we perceive through our emotions. As teachers, we know that student learning is helped or hindered by how students feel during learning periods. If they return from recess upset about a playmate, it is likely they will not be focused on the mathematics lesson you are trying to teach. This is where an aspect of your emotional intelligence kicks in; you'll deliberately find space to give emotional support and help the student transition so they can resume learning. Unsurprisingly, this dynamic also applies to adult relationships. Yes, we have typically learned to recognize and manage our emotions much better than our students because it is practical and adult to do so, but we all know and experience how our emotional state influences how we react, sometimes not in the way we'd like.

Psychologist and relationship expert Daniel Goleman has written extensively about emotional intelligence. His work applies to how we think and act through our emotions. Goleman's work provides a context for increasing skill and ability in managing our thoughts and actions so that we can effectively work with other people. Goleman (2005) describes emotional intelligence as the way we handle ourselves in our people relationships; the way we handle things is based on how we feel and how we manage those feelings. According to Goleman (2019), there are five components of emotional intelligence that work together.

1. **Self-awareness:** People who have self-awareness know their guiding vision and act toward it. They are aware of their feelings and how those might affect their moods or reactions. People who have self-awareness show humor about their mistakes because they can easily look outside themselves to see how their actions in a situation might not have worked so well; they know their limitations.

2. **Self-regulation:** When a person shows self-regulation, it means that they can regulate their behavior. Self-regulation enables the person to choose actions that will help stabilize their behavior. People who demonstrate self-regulation are reflective and comfortable with ambiguity, which lessens the risk of being impulsive or driven by emotions.

3. **Motivation:** People are driven to achieve when they are motivated. But achievement is not for money or power. It is simply a drive to do more. Such people love learning and asking questions. They are not satisfied with a personal status quo but seek to do more, learn more, achieve more. Setbacks aren't viewed as failures, but rather as opportunities for growth.

4. **Empathy:** People who demonstrate empathy show considerations of others' emotions. They care about people. They seek to understand how people are feeling; for example, during times of change or growth, an empathetic person would approach these situations with care for the other. Empathy is a skill that builds relationships with people.

5. **Social skills:** People with social skills build rapport with others, they can find the middle ground in group situations, and they are great at working in teams. People who have this intelligence understand that it's better if we all work together! It's interesting that working on social skills doesn't look like work because it is relationship building. This means that people are talking and spending time with others to make and maintain the connections necessary in social work, which comprises all group work.

Let's focus a little more specifically on the empathy component. According to writer Brené Brown (2021), "Empathy is the most powerful tool of compassion . . . that allows us to understand what someone is experiencing and to reflect back that understanding" (p. 120). Empathy lets you interpret what is happening between people. Being empathetic with a colleague who is under emotional duress allows us to respond in a way that supports them. We rely on three types of empathy in our relationship work, and all three contribute to building relationships (Goleman, McKee, & Achor, 2017).

1. **Cognitive empathy:** Explaining something so that it is meaningful to the other person
2. **Emotional empathy:** Feeling what the person is feeling
3. **Empathetic concern:** Feeling what the other person is feeling and responding in a way to support them

We can learn to be more empathetic by *really* listening, by not judging what is said, by being present and holding our own emotions at bay, and by learning about what another person's experience is like, even if we haven't had a similar experience. According to Brown (2021), we cannot honestly walk in each other's shoes, all we can do is try to understand. When people show empathy to others, it is team building because empathy connects us. When people lack empathy, it is difficult to redeem the quality that is lost. The following sections detail some ways you can improve your emotional intelligence.

Listen

During conversation, how many times have you noticed that people don't listen to each other? They often just present their ideas and, eventually, the person with the more dominant voice convinces people to do something a certain way, while the person who does not feel heard becomes quiet. This is because the stance of a discussion is to convince others of your personal view or agenda.

Teachers are comfortable *telling*—we tell students what to do or tell them how to do something. Telling is the opposite of an inquiry approach to teaching. Learning new teaching practices or approaches and understanding how the brain learns can shift from telling to teaching for meaning. *Listening* is a purposeful leadership skill that can be cultivated (Wefald, 2022). Learning about listening can shift our work with others from telling, to listening, to building connections with other educators. It is a skill that builds relationships and that we can further develop as teacher leaders. Listening to each other also helps us learn more about teaching and leading.

Teachers are busy people who feel a lot of demands placed on them. Being busy can make people feel overwhelmed and diminishes efficacy. When teachers feel heard and supported, they feel valued. Feeling valued builds relationships because it is "the first requisite for undercutting impersonal bureaucratic influences" (Galloway, 1976, p. 316). As we grow in our emotional intelligence and skill, we become aware of our own thoughts and feelings and of other people's needs and how to support them. These are interpersonal connections that need space and time. Such interpersonal connections are not made in day-to-day conversation largely because there is no space for the connections. There is a general feeling that there is no time. What people really need is a conversation where they feel valued. Listening provides just that; it builds relationships and can be empathetic.

Wheatley (2005b) acknowledges this in her work on the value of our relationships, stating, "When people are engaged in meaningful conversation, the whole room reflects curiosity and delight. People move closer physically, their faces exhibit intense listening, and the air becomes charged with their attention to each other" (p. x). As teacher leaders focus on building schools that make a difference, listening and inviting teachers into conversations to learn from each other is important and valuable.

Teachers have a tremendous store of unspoken teaching knowledge. Conversation that promotes listening helps bring our funds of knowledge together—a sharing of understandings and know-how about education. This collegial inquiry in teachers' professional learning is built on our widening lens resulting from meaningful conversations. During these conversations, we are reminded that we have a lot to learn from each other; that the collective wisdom in the room is greater than our own knowledge as teacher leaders (Wheatley, 2005b).

When we listen, we learn what is important to the speaker. This awareness changes perceptions that we may have held about fellow teachers because we might have criticized or judged them for not teaching the way we teach because we think we know better. In coaching, it might be easy to accidentally judge a teacher because they are not meeting the marks. But, if our focus is on building relationships first, we must listen and learn from our fellow teachers. It gives value to their work and acknowledges them as people and members of our teaching community.

The following are some ways to be a good listener.

- Show you are listening by making eye contact, nodding your head in agreement, and keeping an eye on body language.
- Don't be silent; it's OK to talk. Ask clarifying questions about the topic.
- Repeat what you hear, but don't interpret it.
- Monitor your emotions.
- Give thoughtful responses if warranted, but don't try to solve the problem for the person.
- Stay present, stay in the conversation—don't think about what you want to tell them.
- If the conversation needs more time, set up a time to meet again.

Spend Time Together

When we spend time with teachers, we have more opportunities for meaningful conversations with them. We get to know them and see how their teaching practices are uniquely related to who they are and their purposes as educators. We connect on purpose and practice. By being in other teachers' spaces (and having them in ours), we learn that we share the important work of education and the paradigm that good teaching matters. We cannot help but become more respectful of the teachers we work with and aware of the gifts, knowledge, and skills that they have. Remember, teacher leadership is not just about developing the self, but about building the teacher leader capacity of fellow educators.

We build relationships when we recognize and honor the wonderful resources teachers bring. The connection we build increases the potential to create better schools because of our combined efforts and focus on student learning.

Some relationship-building ideas include the following.

- Plan time together. Set up a regular time to meet. It could be before school or ten minutes before or after a required meeting (such as a staff meeting).
- Have lunch together. Plan to talk about topics related to practice.
- Celebrate student learning by inviting teachers into your classroom. For example, celebrate the completion of student narrative writing by inviting teachers to your room as guests or have your students visit teachers' rooms to read their finished writings.
- Have fun together. Go get a cup of coffee or plan to take a walk after school.

Be Respectful

We don't really talk about respect among professionals in schools. It is apparent that teachers respect each other by the way they share and work together: "When all the adults serve as models of respect and work to make their colleagues feel appreciated for their impact on the school community, everyone will benefit—including the students" (Quaglia & Lande, 2016, p. 28). When it comes to respect, teacher's perspectives and voices need to be heard. After all, teachers have the unique position of working within school and among students, from which they have gained valuable knowledge and insight. Listening is respectful. Sometimes it seems like there is no time, and when this happens, we might present as being rushed or in a hurry. This might seem like we were uncivil to someone. In the world of relationships, we can spot respect and disrespect. Feeling a lack of respect cuts to the core.

Here is where emotional intelligence skill development can help. Journaling is a way to promote mindfulness about bumps that happen in the day and to make plans so we can be more positive in the future. Keep a journal to promote self-awareness about when you feel you may have been uncivil to colleagues or other people. Take a minute and respond to the following questions about respect and your work as an educator.

Have you felt a lack of respect for what you bring to your work and to teaching? How can you build self-respect in this regard?

_____

_____

Build and Sustain Healthy Relationships | 89

Have you shown disrespect? What was going on? How can you prevent this in the future?

What can you do to increase others' awareness of your respect for what they bring to your learning spaces? How can you promote respect among your team?

Sometimes, teacher leaders are focused on daily demands—following schedules and assisting students. It could be helpful to bring up the concept of respect for the people you work with. Enlist help from your colleagues to ask what makes them feel respected. You might be surprised to learn how they feel about their educational environment. This information can help you, as an agent of change, take action to make things better for teachers and students. Such change can promote thriving at work. It also might help you learn about your own shortcomings in relationships that you did not perceive. As a teacher leader developing emotional intelligence at work, being comfortable with a 360-degree view of who we are is a growth opportunity. Feedback helps us develop awareness of the practices we need to improve on to change for the better.

Be Present

Although spending time together sounds great, the caveat is that you need to be present—physically and mentally. Being present means that your body language shows you are interested and that your mind is still. We can be physically present, yet our minds might be wondering about our after-school plans or about what we might say rather than listening to what is being said. Being present takes mental practice because our feelings push our brains to think through our emotions, which is distracting.

The following are some suggestions for being present.

- Take a calming breath before you meet with teachers and think about the purpose of your visit or conversation. Remind yourself that relationships move practice together.

- Watch your body language. Be careful about crossing your arms or putting your hands on your hips. Be mindful of what you are doing. If you feel your arms starting to cross, stop them! Instead, open your hands and lay them on your legs. Smile and nod. Give positive eye contact.

- Monitor how other teachers are acting. Are they crossing their arms or frowning? Listen for their tone of voice. It is here where the skills developed through honing your emotional intelligence are needed. Do not react. Pay attention. What is really going on? What might seem like a reaction is really communication. The teacher's body language lets you know that the conversation or your presence is making them feel good or bad about something. When this happens, remember it is not about you—unless you plow ahead as if their feelings don't matter.

- Do not multitask. (No cell phone surfing!)
- Be mindful of yourself, the people around you, and the environment you are in. Be available to the person you are with.

We build connections by being around other people and by being visible ourselves. When teacher leaders help others, they demonstrate that they care and that doing so is worthy of their time and energy. It also demonstrates that we need each other—that our relationships are integral to our collective work. Helping out is another way to be positive. It's a way of sharing your energy and joy about being in education.

Build Trust

Trust is built on a sustained relationship with someone. We work on building trust through our actions, what we say (including what we say about a teachers' work and who we say it to), and how we control our emotions when things get heated. It is built through self-regulation—the ability to control our emotions when things are intense. Trust is built on forgiveness and acceptance that the other person is doing their best. Teacher leadership is "not about role, but rather performing actions that enable teachers to earn the trust of their peers and lead school improvement efforts" (Lambert, 2003, p. 13). The framework of teacher leadership involves building relationships that are outcome oriented, not role directed. Trust can be repaired when it is damaged, but it takes time and effort to invest in rebuilding relationships.

The following are some ways to establish trust.

- Be authentic with others, let people know who you are, and that you're like them. Your work together involves being vulnerable about your own learning. Showing vulnerability about not having all the answers and working together to learn is a way to build trust.
- Keep your commitments. Break your habit of responding yes immediately; tell people you'll get back to them after you check your planner.
- Show up to events when you say you'll be there. If you promise to bring materials, bring them.
- Apologize.
- Remember that trust takes time.

Honor Others' Voices

We all have talents and viewpoints. It is not uncommon when teachers work together that someone shares what they do or something they created to support student learning. Treat this as a gift and show gratitude. Honor the contributions of fellow teachers to other teachers—mention their names. In schools, where power is in relationships, build your relationships by acknowledging their work, creativity, and the product they shared. Give credit to the person who had a great idea or created a project to support learning. "To feel included in the larger family of the school and to identify with the recognition of others" (Galloway, 1976, p. 318) creates an environment where we celebrate each other and move forward together in building interpersonal relationships.

Honoring others' voices is important in building equity-focused schools. Teachers of different cultures, experiences, and life stories bring with them varying worldviews and ways of seeing how actions impact their roles in education. Building relationships among teachers also means that we learn more about our world, the histories of education, and the cultures of people. One way to learn more with others is through book clubs (chapter 3, page 51).

The following are some helpful ways to honor your colleagues' voices.

- Publicly acknowledge them for what they did or created.
- Write a thank you note or email.
- Show gratitude when talking about what you learned from them.
- If you use their work or tweak it for your own use, give praise by referencing them as the source of your idea.
- Be gentle with people. Ignore small mistakes!

Communicate Effectively

The teacher leaders' work of relationship building occurs alongside the work of building teacher learning and teaching capacity. This is accomplished as teachers work together in professional inquiries. As agents of change, sometimes we engage in challenging conversations to raise the bar about dialogue and practice. It is difficult to have such conversations when they are not part of the status quo (Mangin, 2010). The work is to provide and build knowledge and practice so that teachers can shift their beliefs toward a more effective method or strategy that is good for students and can bring more equity-centered teaching practices. Teachers aren't used to hard feedback and teacher leaders might not be comfortable giving it. But it all comes back to empathy and emotional intelligence. Stepping back and focusing on the goal of the feedback—to help our practices promote student learning—helps us convey the message with empathy rather than judgment.

The following are some ways to communicate more effectively.

- Plan what you are going to say before you talk.
- Pay attention to your voice tone and enthusiasm. Think about using different voice levels as you talk.
- Ask people if they have questions about what you are saying.
- Be clear about what you are trying to say, and don't repeat yourself. If you are repetitive, it helps to write your major points down before you talk.

Conclusion

Relationships are key to our important work as teacher leaders. We need to be co-builders of growth-oriented learning communities for teachers and students. We need connections. Our relationships are mutually sustaining when we work on them together and give this precious connection the grace and patience to grow.

Relationships provide the emotional space we work within. We build this foundation with others by developing skills in understanding our own emotions and actions toward others that invite the relationship. As teacher leaders, we share this important educational work. Student learning is key and working together in communities that focus on this is paramount. We know that knowledge is created within the person (or student) through engagement and that "knowledge never exists independently of this process of my being in relationship with an event, an idea, another person . . . knowledge is created in relationship" (Wheatley, 2005a, p. 122). For teacher leaders, relationships are life-giving to our leadership.

Reflecting on My Reactions

Name: _____

Date: _____

Instructions: Please fill in your reactions to your feelings according to a particular situation on the Likert scale from 1 (positive reaction) to 5 (negative reaction). Think about what made you feel that way. How did your feelings affect the situation? If you were to do it all over again, how would you respond?

My reaction to feeling anxious: _____
_____

1	2	3	4	5
Positive	Somewhat Positive	Neutral	Somewhat Negative	Negative
○	○	○	○	○

My reaction to feeling angry: _____
_____

1	2	3	4	5
Positive	Somewhat Positive	Neutral	Somewhat Negative	Negative
○	○	○	○	○

My reaction to feeling sad: _____
_____

1	2	3	4	5
Positive	Somewhat Positive	Neutral	Somewhat Negative	Negative
○	○	○	○	○

The Emerging Teacher Leader © 2024 Solution Tree Press • SolutionTree.com
Visit **go.SolutionTree.com/leadership** to download this free reproducible.

Chapter 5
TAKE CARE OF YOURSELF

We need resilience and hope and a spirit that can carry us through the doubt and fear. We need to believe that we can effect change.

—Brené Brown

light attendants emphasize that you need to put on your own oxygen mask first before assisting others. Similarly, teachers need to take care of themselves to effectively lead others. Teaching is a dynamic, complex process. To teach and lead well, we need to build our resilience and build resilience in our students. As teacher leaders, we also need to support our colleagues. Resilience, self-care, a work-life balance, and an affirmation that teaching is a learning process all support healthy teachers and their work. Taking care of yourself is the fifth dynamic practice of teacher leadership.

This chapter explores the importance of resilience, self-care, and work-life balance to sustain teachers during their professional tenure. It also asks teachers to reflect on their practice and consider, "Am I thriving?" Healthy teachers result from schools that thrive (Collie & Perry, 2019). We will explore strategies that teachers can use to alleviate work overload and thrive, the social-emotional impact of teachers on their students, and the need for teachers to care for their own social-emotional wellness so they can be present and ready to teach others.

Avoiding Overwhelm

Stress, including the feeling that it is hard to manage the complexities of teaching, is very real for educators. The job's demands are far-reaching and can be overwhelming. Sometimes, this can lead to utter exhaustion and a reduced sense of teaching efficacy (Elster et al., 2022). When teachers are asked to prepare their students for high achievement while taking on ever-greater workloads with fewer resources, this overload can take a toll on personal well-being, and the stress can lead to teacher burnout. Burnout is an acute stress; it occurs when one is emotionally drained and unable to keep up with the demands of work. All teachers, including veteran teachers, facing new or higher demands are at risk (Nygaard, 2019). It is important to note that stress is manageable—just because a teacher feels stressed does not mean that they have burnout. People who are burned out are at a high degree of stress and need a quick remedy (Chang, 2009; Ghanizadeh & Jahedizadeh, 2015).

Developing resilience is an integral part of preventing and managing educators' stress. Resilience involves developing coping mechanisms that enable teacher leaders to bounce back from challenging situations or rough days, giving them the strength to manage adversity (Hascher, Beltman, & Mansfield, 2021). This can involve developing a growth mindset (see chapter 6, page 117) or a can-do attitude, practicing gratitude or mindfulness, engaging in positive self-talk, and fostering creativity (Aguilar, 2018). These practices increase our capacity to manage emotions through adversity and keep going, even when things get tough.

As a teacher leader, you can learn all the latest teaching techniques, plan amazing lessons, establish effective classroom management, and collaborate with colleagues. Yet, to manage the facets of teacher leadership and to flourish as a leader, you need a high level of emotional resilience. We know that teaching is challenging. The attrition rate of new teachers is about 50 percent in the first five years (Aguilar, 2018), and the attraction to this profession has somewhat dimmed due to poor wages and demands on teachers (Doherty, 2020). The teaching workforce needs to be more robust. School districts must act now to improve teacher retention rates. Furthermore, although teacher training programs have contributed to skill development in how to teach, there is a lack of resilience-focused curriculum in teacher preparation programs (Mansfield, Beltman, Weatherby-Fell, & Broadley, 2016).

Knowing the obstacles can help teacher leaders take action to maintain and promote resilience. Let's identify some adverse circumstances teacher leaders might face that challenge resilience.

Time

The most frequent challenge that we hear from teachers all over the world is a lack of time. It is not uncommon to hear, "I don't have time to plan, time to do everything I want to do, and time to differentiate and meet the needs of all my students." It's hard to accept the fact that you will never have as much time as you would like. Time is a precious commodity for us all. Accept that you will never have as much time or as many resources as you would like. Perfectionism is a time-taker. A constant quest for perfectionism may be your enemy and work against you. There is no such thing as the perfect lesson plan or the perfect teacher. Let's focus on our students and why we're teaching rather than on how our job performance looks. Also don't forget the importance of collaborating with colleagues. Although it takes time to meet with your colleagues, it also saves time. You can divide and conquer the workload. The acronym of TEAM is true: Together Everyone Achieves More.

It is critical that we stay organized so that we streamline what we do. Consider the phrase, "work smarter, not harder." Instead of myriad to-do lists, keep a *ta-dah* list and celebrate your accomplishments as you finish them! Start small and keep going—remember, small changes lead to bigger ones. As a teacher leader, it is not necessary to change everything you are doing. It's OK to start slowly (like the fable of the tortoise and the hare)—implementing an idea or two at a time—rather than throwing out everything you are doing. Regular progress is the goal of your professional journey.

Balance

Remember to seek and keep balance in your life. Your professional career as an educational leader is important, but don't forget to take time for yourself, your family, and your friends. It is easy to feel overwhelmed at times when preparing lesson plans and differentiating them to meet your students' individual needs. But when you have balance, the joy of teaching shines through when you're present.

The challenge of finding balance compounds if you find yourself in a difficult classroom environment. Reflect on the following questions to self-determine the level of balance (or imbalance) in your teaching life.

What do you find most challenging in the classroom?

_____
_____
_____
_____
_____
_____

Do you remember a specific event that was particularly difficult? Why do you think that was? How did the experience make you stronger?

_____
_____
_____
_____
_____
_____

At times, classroom behavior management is challenging, but even veteran teachers experience this and may struggle to manage a particular class. You might remember when it was difficult to help a particular student or group of students whose behaviors didn't match your skill set. The good news is that you are a learner, and you can learn from books and your colleagues to better understand your students' needs and effective classroom management strategies. As your repertoire of strategies broadens through experience and learning, your resilience grows because of increased confidence. Situations that were problematic tend to become less frequent.

Resilient educators know what's important, and act in accordance with their values. When your decisions are aligned with your values, decision-making moments become opportunities to connect with what's most important, rather than a drain on your resolve.

Workload

Educators cite the hefty workload of teaching as another challenge that interferes with their happiness and effectiveness. Teaching is an incredibly important and complex job. It takes a significant amount of energy to think about what our students need to move forward in their learning. We spend time evaluating student work, writing and grading assessments, lesson planning, prepping, and setting up for the many lessons that are taught weekly. Days fill up, and so do our work hours. In this scenario we can lean into collegial inquiry to streamline our work. It also gives us opportunity to collaborate and focus on student learning needs rather than seeing lesson planning as the end goal.

Trends in education are constantly evolving—so are new school or districtwide programs and innovations that contribute to teacher workload. One way to combat the resulting initiative fatigue is to focus on *practices* and not *programs*. When you are able to evaluate new or existing initiatives, ask your school-based team the following questions.

- What is the desired outcome of the program?
- What would you see as evidence of implementation? (Three to five ideas.)
- What do teachers gain by implementing these practices?
- What obstacles might impede implementation of these practices? How will this program be launched?
- What kind of ongoing support will be needed for implementation?

Through this process, your team might realize that this program is not needed or that you already have the skills to achieve the desired outcomes. Perhaps instructional coaching may be needed instead of adopting a packaged program. Investing in new programs requires time and energy. Perhaps it would be better to develop the efficacy and skills needed to manage challenges related to student learning. Curriculum comes and goes. Remember, teachers are not programs; we are teachers, and we desire to teach (Leiter & Maslach, 2024).

Supporting Resilience

A study documented that teachers who had the highest levels of well-being and job satisfaction and the lowest levels of burnout, also had relatively high levels of self-esteem, self-care, emotional intelligence, and an optimistic outlook (Ainsworth & Oldfield, 2019). So, if teachers are to make self-care a priority, how do they incorporate different self-care elements into the day?

To begin, there are some basics that may seem obvious but are nonetheless important. It is vital to make sure that you get sufficient sleep, eat well, and engage in some form of regular exercise (Ainsworth & Oldfield, 2019). Keeping a written schedule helps. For example, to prioritize exercise, some people write their after-school workout in their teacher planner, so they leave school on time rather than work late and miss exercising.

The following are some tips to build emotional resilience in the teaching profession.

- **Know yourself and how your emotions can make you feel about yourself:** Keep your purpose and passion in mind. Take precious time to reflect on how you feel. What brings you joy? (Aguilar, 2018). Recognizing and naming emotions can powerfully boost resilience. Tune in and get clear about what you are feeling—be able to identify and describe the emotions.
- **Set realistic goals:** Seek daily and weekly goals that may be challenging but are also doable, achievable, and believable. Goals will also help build your confidence because when you meet each goal, you have a small win. How do you make your goals doable? By breaking them down into smaller, achievable steps and celebrating every step of the way!
- **Tell positive, empowering stories that uplift you and your students:** The stories we tell ourselves and others are important. It really makes a difference how we view, interpret, and talk about events that happen. Having uplifting stories about teaching helps us cultivate our resilience. End each day with a small mindful moment by telling yourself something you liked about your day.
- **Build healthy habits:** Develop healthy habits so that you are physically able to be present and compassionate with others. It is vital

to take care of your physical health by getting enough sleep, eating well, and exercising. Self-care is essential for resilience. Do things that bring you joy and relaxation.

- **Be mindful (focus on the now):** Work on being in the present moment without dreading the future or regretting the past. Remembering past hurts and offenses just brings up negative emotions. And, when you remember small hurts, it hurts your emotional self all over again. Don't forget to press the pause button for some mindful breathing or brief meditation time.

- **Focus on the positive:** Pay more attention to what is working rather than what is not. Our brains are wired to see negative threats (Aguilar, 2018). For instance, when working with students, try to catch them being good instead of hyperfocusing on negative behaviors. Focus on the great things you are doing too!

- **Practice compassionate thinking:** When we cultivate compassionate reactions to ourselves and others, we become better equipped to handle difficult situations. This involves broadening our perspective about a situation and learning to empathize with others.

- **Be a lifelong learner:** Be curious! Resilient teachers have deep curiosity and desire to learn. They ask themselves: What can I learn from this situation? Reflect on your own learning processes and begin to see challenges as invitations to curiosity.

- **Play and create with your students:** We all need play because it is enjoyable. Being immersed in play can unlock resources for dealing with stress and solving problems by helping us look at different approaches to facing challenges. Don't forget to build play and creativity into your day.

- **Be open to the change process:** In education, change is inevitable. One of the constants in education is change—the other is lack of resources. The school year can bring about all kinds of changes; be prepared for them so that you aren't thrown off track. As a teacher leader, you are an agent of change. Remain calm and evaluate situations to determine which responses will have the greatest impact. Be proactive in the change process. Instead of seeing change as an obstacle, see it as an opportunity for growth.

- **Celebrate with gratitude:** Being grateful centers us. Don't forget to take time to celebrate your own accomplishments as well as your students' and your colleagues'. Developing a daily attitude of gratitude will also build your resilience.
- **Learn to say no:** This is difficult to accomplish, particularly for teacher leaders. Teacher leaders like to be involved in school. Most of us are used to being helpers and people pleasers. We say yes too often to help people out. This does not serve our own self-care and just adds to our busyness. Before taking on another task, hit the pause button. How is your energy load?
- **Interact with someone you don't typically interact with:** Make new connections to broaden your view of your school community. Take time to interact with a student, parent, colleague, or other staff member and broaden your social circle. Why? Because a sense of community is critical for resilience.
- **Seek out coaches and mentors:** A coach or mentor can give you another perspective about your teaching practice. A mentor or a coach is like having a mirror who also gives you support and feedback. Increased skill and confidence build resilience, which promotes your teacher leadership work.
- **Set boundaries and leave work at work:** Leaving work is difficult because teaching is connected to our passion. We care deeply about our students and their families. Sometimes, we bring home our emotions, tension, and exhaustion; at that point, it might be time for a self-check. We need to set boundaries when our work is leaking into our personal life.

Build Self-Esteem

Self-esteem is also an important factor in resilience (Bissessar, 2014). Recognizing potential daily threats to our self-esteem helps us be cognizant of them when they occur (Ainsworth & Oldfield, 2019). This way we can be prepared to understand why we might feel defeated or frustrated from time to time. Education consultant Dennis Lawrence (1999) identifies common threats to teachers' self-esteem, including dealing with challenging parents, being observed in the classroom, lack of positive feedback from administrators, and handling students' defiant behavior.

Do these sound familiar? While these threats cannot completely be avoided, understanding how these factors might undermine our self-esteem is important. These sources of stress are often transient and fleeting, but their effects linger. What can we do when they crop up? Try to press the pause button and create little events throughout the week that lift our self-esteem and joy. Think about being grateful, something you are looking forward to, or what went well. Some people place these musings in their lesson planner at the end of the day or week, keeping the focus on the positive work they're doing.

Improve School Culture

The phrase "happy teachers make happy schools" means that self-care and resilience do not stop with individual teachers—they need to be a schoolwide focus. It has been found that school culture thrives when teachers are given time to collaborate with other teachers and establish doable goals (Goodwin & Shebby, 2020). This schoolwide culture that promotes students' success aligns with Hattie's work on collective efficacy and student achievement (Hattie, 2023). Understanding your emotions and what strategies work best to support them begins with being in touch with your own bandwidth. The following questions can help you think more about how this concept ties into your school culture.

Consider the aspects of your school's work that most sap your energy and bandwidth. Which ones result from policies, practices, or conventions in your school that could realistically change?

_____
_____
_____
_____
_____
_____
_____

*W*hat can you do to make that change happen?

_____
_____
_____
_____
_____
_____
_____

*W*hat are some ways you could set up guardrails to protect you from having your energy sapped and limit interruptions to protect time for concentrated work?

_____
_____
_____
_____
_____
_____
_____
_____

*W*hy do you think that many schools suffer from initiative overload and fatigue?

_____
_____
_____

_____

_____

_____

_____

Reducing Stress

It is essential that we address teacher stress because of the negative effect on both the teacher and the students. When teachers feel overwhelmed, they might not act the way they envisioned themselves to be as teachers. This may be demonstrated by impatience with students, less creativity in their teaching approach, fewer positive relationships with other staff members, and less risk-taking as classroom teachers. These factors can also lead to negative outcomes for students, including decreased engagement, lower academic achievement, and unmotivated learners (Van Ryzin & Roseth, 2021). Managing stress is essential for teachers' well-being and resilience, as well as their students' success. Stress is a major concern for educators as chronicled by teacher turnover rate data (Farmer, 2020). Too much stress can lead to burnout; this extreme stress affects the person and, ultimately, everyone around them.

Being aware of your stress level and being proactive with strategies helps manage stress. When you alleviate stress, you are happier at work and teach with more focus and enthusiasm. By being proactive in managing stress, your overall well-being will improve as well as job satisfaction. A multifaceted approach is needed to properly take care of your emotional, physical, and mental health to manage stress effectively.

What are some causes of stress for you in the classroom? How do these connect to your emotions? Take a moment to reflect on the following prompts.

I feel stressed when . . .

_____

_____

_____

I feel angry when...

I feel sad when...

As you reflect on your answers, consider the following techniques that can help manage stress.

- **Physical exercise:** Exercise is a terrific way to reduce stress levels and improve your physical health (Edenfield & Blumenthal, 2011). It does not have to be too strenuous or a major workout—even a walk outside or a yoga class will help.
- **Mindfulness and meditation:** You can be mindful, in the present moment, experiencing the sights, sounds, and smells around you. This practice will help you become more centered, calmer, and can reduce your stress levels (Barbor, 2001).

- **Deep breathing:** This is a simple and much-needed activity that you can do at any time, even outside during playground duty. Focus on your breath as it enters and leaves your body. Similar to meditation, this practice can help you feel calmer and less stressed (Perciavalle et al., 2017). Breathe in deeply through your nose. It might help to put one hand on your chest and the other on your belly so you can feel the impact of the process. Allow your belly to expand as you exhale. Exhale through your mouth so you can feel your belly contract. Repeat this process until you feel calm and centered. To add to the relaxing mood, lower the lights or play some soft music in the background.

- **Body awareness and muscle relaxation:** This technique can help you reduce your stress, relax your muscles, and brighten up your overall well-being (Davis, Eshelman, & McKay, 2008). To practice this technique, focus on your breathing and release any negative thoughts or emotions you might have. Then, notice how your body feels. What muscles feel tense? With practice and the focus on relaxation, you will gain a deeper awareness of your body and learn to let go of tension and stress easily.

- **Guided imagery:** This technique can improve your focus (Bigham, McDannel, Luciano, & Salgado-Lopez, 2014). The strategy involves forming vivid mental images to promote relaxation and positive emotions. The process is quite simple. Find a quiet place and close your eyes. After a few deep breaths to relax your body, visualize a calming scene—maybe a beach or a park. Then, imagine yourself in this environment and let go of your worries and stress. Another extension to this process is to visualize a specific outcome for a specific situation—it might be an upcoming presentation you are giving or interactions with a difficult student. This technique can also be used with other techniques; not only will these reduce stress, but they can improve concentration and focus (Zemla, Sedek, Wróbel, Postepski, & Wojcik, 2023).

Give yourself time to pause and reflect and do some quick-write reflections on your role and work-life balance. The "Action Plan for Wellness Worksheet" reproducible at the end of this chapter (page 109) can help you consider ways to deal with challenges, and the "Wellness Check-In" (page 113) can help you ascertain your wellness strengths and areas for improvement. Reflection boosts creativity and provides a sense of awareness and calm. These pages are meant for you, the teacher leader, because you deserve to set aside time for yourself. Writing and reflecting are perfect channels for introspection. You begin to appreciate new things, and writing about your accomplishments can boost your self-esteem (Walker, 2013). Search your heart for the answers.

Conclusion

Taking care of yourself first is a sign of strong leadership. It is important for teacher leaders to keep their health and wellness in mind. Model work-life balance and good health for your students and colleagues. It is time to demonstrate that a healthy teacher promotes health all around. Keep your priorities in perspective and reclaim your energy, passion, joy, and time.

Action Plan for Wellness Worksheet

Create three actions or strategies to help you realize your optimum wellness. Identify a potential challenge and then make an action plan to carry out.

Challenge: What challenges are you facing? How do these challenges impact you? Why did you choose to address these challenges?

Action or strategy: What specifically are you going to do to help overcome these challenges? What help do you need from others? What do you need to learn? What resources might you need? How often do you need to take this action or strategy? Provide some needed details.

Data point: How will you measure this? How will you know if you are successful?

Evaluation: How well did you accomplish this? (Be honest.)

Action 1 Challenge:

_____
_____
_____
_____
_____
_____

Action or Strategy:

_____
_____
_____
_____
_____
_____

Data Point:

_____

Evaluation:

_____

Action 2 Challenge:

_____

Action or Strategy:

_____

Data Point:

Evaluation:

Action 3 Challenge:

Action or Strategy:

Data Point:

Evaluation:

Wellness Check-In

For each category of wellness, rate the following.

Social Wellness

How do you rate your present social wellness?

Low									High
1	2	3	4	5	6	7	8	9	10

Provide rationale for choosing this level of wellness:

_____
_____
_____
_____

Emotional Wellness

How do you rate your present emotional wellness?

Low									High
1	2	3	4	5	6	7	8	9	10

Provide rationale for choosing this level of wellness:

_____
_____
_____
_____

Occupational Wellness

How do you rate your present occupational wellness?

Low									High
1	2	3	4	5	6	7	8	9	10

Provide rationale for choosing this level of wellness:

_____
_____
_____
_____

Intellectual Wellness

How do you rate your present intellectual wellness?

Low									High
1	2	3	4	5	6	7	8	9	10

Provide rationale for choosing this level of wellness:

_____
_____
_____
_____

Physical Wellness

How do you rate your present physical wellness?

Low									High
1	2	3	4	5	6	7	8	9	10

Provide rationale for choosing this level of wellness:

_____
_____
_____
_____

Spiritual Wellness

How do you rate your present spiritual wellness?

Low									High
1	2	3	4	5	6	7	8	9	10

Provide rationale for choosing this level of wellness:

_____
_____
_____
_____

The Emerging Teacher Leader © 2024 Solution Tree Press • SolutionTree.com
Visit **go.SolutionTree.com/leadership** to download this free reproducible.

Chapter 6
CULTIVATE A GROWTH MINDSET

A change from believing there are limits to learning, and life, to believing that anything can be learned or achieved is a change from a fixed to a growth mindset.

—Jo Boaler

Teaching is a dynamic and demanding profession, but being a teacher leader adds another layer to the complexity. This is because as teacher leaders develop, the relational and knowledge-based work they do compels them to push outside of their classroom boundaries—all for the betterment of their schools and students. What teacher leaders believe about their developing leadership capacity is important. It is vital that teacher leaders cultivate and nurture a growth mindset—the sixth and final practice of teacher leadership.

In this chapter, we will review and explore growth mindset and student learning. We will address this concept as it relates to teacher leadership (and very likely, all leadership). Sustaining your work as a teacher leader and having a growth mindset about teacher leadership learning go hand in hand.

To start off, let's think about what you already know about mindset. Take a minute to respond to the following prompts.

*D*o you think that you can learn anything if you put your mind to it?

___

*I*s there something that you are timid about learning or trying? Why or why not?

___

*H*ave you given up on doing something that you wanted to do? What held you back?

___

According to Carol S. Dweck, we create beliefs about things based on our experiences with them (Dweck, 2007). These implicit belief ideas get linked together with our goals and how we behave into a *meaning system*. They are implicit because people do not know that they hold these beliefs, yet they use them for sensemaking in their daily lives (Molden & Dweck, 2006). The organizing component of this meaning system is called our *mindset*. This is to say that "mindsets create meaning systems" (Dweck & Yeager, 2019, p. 483) that we use to frame our effort, persistence, motivation, and how we act (Dweck, 2007; Nalipay, King, Mordeno, Chai, & Jong, 2021). Your mindset is the way you frame what you will do or how you might approach something in any number of areas.

You might have heard about various mindsets, such as a student mindset about learning, or mathematics (Boaler, 2019; Bui, Pongsakdi, McMullen, Lehtinen, & Hannula-Sormunen, 2023; Dweck, 2007; Rege et al., 2021; Sun, 2018; Yeager & Dweck, 2012), teacher mindset (Frondozo, King, Nalipay, & Mordeno, 2020; Jonsson, Beach, Korp, & Erlandson, 2012; Mesler, Corbin, & Martin, 2021; Nalipay et al., 2021; Yeager et al., 2022), and leadership mindset (Chase, 2010; Gottfredson & Reina, 2021). Dweck's mindset theory has broadened to new domains, in all facets of life (Dweck & Yeager, 2019). There has even been discussion about how mindset works with stereotypes and social awareness. For example, it was found that the way high schoolers acted toward others could change as they developed a growth mindset about certain social qualities, such as being a winner or loser (Dweck & Yeager, 2019).

The rhetoric about mindset has broadened contextually as well. Mindsets have been explored in the contexts in which they are demonstrated, such as in workplaces or business (Berg, Wrzesniewski, Grant, Kurkoski, & Welle, 2023; Johnston, 2017; Kouzes & Posner, 2019; Murphy & Reeves, 2019; Rattan & Ozgumus, 2021) and in coaching (Chase, 2010; Dweck, 2009; Lowery, 2019). The overall message is simple; change the beliefs that hold you back, and you can change your life (Boaler, 2019). In other words, there is a limitlessness to what we can learn and do. This idea holds true in all aspects of our development, including teaching and teacher leadership.

Understand Growth and Fixed Mindsets

Through her extensive research, Dweck and colleagues have identified that given different domains (for example, intelligence and athleticism) our mindsets "are on a continuum, anchored at one end by those with a fixed mindset . . . and at the other end by those with growth mindset" (Dweck et al., 1995, as cited in Kouzes & Posner, 2019, p. 830). Dweck explains that "A *growth mindset* is the belief that human capacities are not fixed but can be developed over time" (Dweck & Yeager, 2019, p. 481) and a *fixed mindset* is the belief that one's abilities and intelligence is fixed and cannot be improved (Dweck, 2007). The two views are distinctly different in how they approach learning. A growth mindset is malleable, and people (their intelligence, ability, attributes) can grow over time with effort. Meanwhile, a fixed mindset means that we are born with the abilities or traits that make us who we are. For example, in sports, a fixed mindset would believe that star athletes are born, not made. On the other hand, a growth mindset approach would hold a foundational belief that great athletes are developed through hard work, commitment, and persistence (Dweck, 2009).

This presence of fixed mindset and growth mindset intervention has been explored in a variety of areas through research (Bui et al., 2023; Esparza, Shumow, & Schmidt, 2014; Yeager & Dweck, 2012). Let's look at mathematics to explain the differences between these mindsets. According to Dweck (2007), students (and teachers) can hold a view that people are either good or bad at mathematics, and that is why they do or do not achieve. For example, students with a fixed mindset believe that their own intelligence and abilities are innate and do not change. They worry about not looking smart to their peers, get upset by making mistakes, and give up easily. This means that they truly feel stuck and that they can't improve in mathematics, even if they try. However, students with a growth mindset understand that their ability can change through effort and practice; they don't give up. Remember, there is a caveat about student effort—sheer effort will not necessarily increase student learning and achievement. And praise for effort when effort is not working creates a false growth mindset, which leads students in the opposite direction of growth (Dweck, 2007; Dweck & Yeager, 2019).

Students with a growth mindset seek help from others in their quest to understand more and to gather other approaches that will help them be successful at learning (Dweck, 2007). Mistakes and challenges are not obstacles. Instead, challenges are meaningful because they need to be solved. In other words, they are action oriented to learning. In mathematics, a growth mindset can be cultivated through mindset interventions (Degol, Wang, Zhang, & Allerton, 2018; Rege et al., 2021). The teacher's role matters in helping students develop a growth mindset.

The importance of a teacher's own mindset about students' learning cannot be overstated. Time and again, research has demonstrated that what teachers think about their students' ability and intelligence can impact students' mindset and learning (Mesler et al., 2021; Moore & Shaughnessy, 2012; Yeager et al., 2022). And, like students, a teacher's mindset about the malleability of their own teaching leads to motivation and persistence in bettering their teaching practice (Nalipay et al., 2021). When it comes to teacher leadership, it makes sense that a growth mindset will sustain leadership development because your own growth, and that of the teachers and students around you, will not move forward without it.

Teacher Mindset About Student Learning

Good teaching matters! We talked about the importance of reflecting on our purpose story and how knowing why we teach drives our pursuit to be great educators in chapter 1 (page 5). We know that teaching well and bettering our practices begin in the classroom (chapter 2, page 27) and, through ongoing learning and collaboration with others, these collective learning opportunities build teacher leadership and affect our students and schools. Effective teachers make a difference to every student, every day. But it isn't entirely about good grades . . . what matters most is that all students not only learn but also *see themselves as learners*, no matter what the challenge. This means teachers who promote student agency help create students who are curious, capable, and persistent learners.

What teachers think about their students makes a difference. As author and Stanford professor Jo Boaler (2019) says, "teachers hold an incredible amount of influence . . . they can change the pathways of students . . . when they communicate to students that they believe in them" (p. 98). When teachers know that all students can learn, they look for ways to convey this belief to students. It is interesting to think about the emergence of a students' growth or fixed mindset as related to the classroom context. Research by psychology professor David S. Yeager and colleagues (2022) explored the notion that students might have a nascent mindset that emerges in class environments that encourages and facilitates a growth mindset. Teachers nurture this mindset by conveying that mistakes are for learning and set up student work so they feel the success of their efforts. On the other hand, teachers with a fixed mindset may make some students feel they are not the smart ones while others are, that it takes talent to rise to the top, or perhaps they are not a mathematics (or any content) person. In this case, the student's growth mindset doesn't take hold.

What teachers say, the amount and type of feedback they give—do they encourage deeper learning, or are they comfort oriented to the point of "you're doing fine"?—presents their mindset to students, and the work and practices of classroom learning and feedback are ways teachers' mindset (growth or not) influences student learning (Mesler et al., 2021; Yeager & Dweck, 2012). What we say to students is important; students can perceive our messages, so what we say and do is related to student achievement (Mesler et al., 2021; Vestad & Bru, 2023). A teacher's mindset can "influence the amount and type of feedback they provide" (Mesler et al., 2021, p. 3). This means that how you perceive your students' learning success and ability, what you do and say, how you teach, what you expect of your students, and how you act on your assumptions about your students' abilities or talents make a difference to every student you teach.

Think about your mindset about the students in your class and their learning. What messages do you give your students? Do you teach them about mindset? Respond to the following prompts.

What are some hidden assumptions you have about the students you teach? This may be visible in how you group students, the expectations you have about them, or who you challenge.

_____
_____
_____
_____
_____
_____
_____

What do you do to help a student who gives up? How do you approach this situation? What are you mindful of?

_____
_____
_____

Cultivate a Growth Mindset | 123

_____
_____
_____
_____

What supports do you give to enable students to be learners? What does skill or conceptual development look like to you?

_____
_____
_____
_____
_____
_____
_____

How do you praise your students? Do you reward them? If so, how and what for?

_____
_____
_____
_____
_____
_____
_____

How do you challenge students? How do you enable them to set their own goals?

_____
_____
_____
_____
_____
_____
_____

Every student needs a teacher who knows and believes they are a learner! An interesting thing about mindset is that people can have different mindsets in different domains. For example, I might have a fixed mindset about replacing the tire on my car, and the challenge of a flat tire is too much for me. I either give up easily or don't try effectively to fix it. I may think that I'll never be able to replace a tire. Yet, I can learn how to replace my car's tire, build my skill, and change my mindset that I can do it. Similarly, students can have different mindsets in different areas. As teachers, it is important not to assume that a student can't learn or has low ability in any area. Teachers must promote a growth mindset and provide opportunity for skill and deep learning, challenge, and goal setting so that all students can achieve learning and tap into their growth mindsets—no matter what the domain.

Teacher Mindset About Teaching

We know that what teachers convey to their students about learning ability and success relates to student growth mindsets. Teachers who focus on students' learning and belief in themselves as learners build learning capacity in their students. Great teachers have growth mindsets, too, related to their own teaching practice (Jonsson et al., 2012). A teachers' growth mindset is the driver for those who seek to design learning experiences that involve problem solving and critical thinking, promote student agency in learning, or professional learning that supports better teaching. This internal belief is not purely about learning new concepts professionally; it is connected to a teacher's ownership of a vision that education matters and that all students can and will learn. A teacher's continuous education about different facets of teaching, learning, emotional growth, and many other areas comes out as their passion. It isn't unfocused passion, but a high level of motivation and persistence to understand teaching more fully. The growth mindset of these teachers is felt as they "enjoy their work and [are] more engaged and committed" (Zilka, Nussbaum, & Bogler, 2023, p. 368). When teachers learn more and increase their teaching efficacy, they become better at teaching.

Great teachers continually seek answers to questions and acquire skills to better their teaching because, ultimately, teacher learning impacts student learning. This kind of learning doesn't happen by chance. It requires ongoing effort and motivation to change or refine what you are doing. Curiosity is important in this endeavor because it provides the spark that connects what we know and the possibilities of what we do not yet know. Reflection is key in the continuous inquiry and improvement that a growth mindset requires. Take time to reflect on your teaching practice, your underlying beliefs about your work, and the effect of this work.

When teachers approach their work with inquiry, they are owners of their own learning. There is agency and an openness to new possibilities. This is growth mindset in action. When did you last ask about your teaching, teaching skill, approach to student learning, or broaden your understanding about new research or development in your content area?

One strategy to help keep the reflective habit going is to choose a day to check in with yourself and tap into the reflection materials that work for your busy life. Some people use journals for reflective writing, but your teacher planner or a calendar also works. Use whatever will be consistent and manageable. Set up a spot in your teacher planner to keep track of your thoughts. Choose a daily or weekly reflection time. What did you question about teaching or student learning? What challenged you? What did you learn about yourself as a teacher? Some people call this your *glows and grows*; the *glows* are where you feel things are working—maybe something you are proud of—and the *grows* are where you might have been challenged. A regular check-in with yourself about your practice makes you look from the outside in.

Here are some prompts to consider for your check-ins.

- Does your teaching practice demonstrate evidence of new learning (your learning)?
- Does any facet of your practice need tweaking? What do you feel when this happens?

- When did you learn something new? What did you do? How did it make you feel? Was the practice sustainable? Why or why not?
- Are you teaching the same lessons year after year? Are your teaching approaches stale and outdated? Are you setting your students up to be self-driven learners?
- How can you turn a teaching challenge into a growth opportunity?
- Are you a teacher learner? What do you need to do to make space for learning? What do you need to do to learn more? What areas beckon you to learn?

Your own mindset as a teacher can be growth or fixed. Mindset comes into play when we teach. Those with a growth mindset are not afraid of challenge; it is enjoyable to seek answers to questions—such enjoyment is engagement. The quest to seek answers from others is growth oriented, while not seeking help is fixed. Researchers Marjolein C. J. Caniëls, Judith H. Semeijn, and Irma H. M. Renders (2018) suggest that "growth mindset is related to work engagement" (p. 52).

To teachers with a growth mindset about teaching, setbacks appear as challenges and opportunities for growth and innovation are possible. Previously, we described teacher leaders as seekers of professional learning who better their teaching practices and are focused on student success. We also talked about the importance of collaboration and participation as co-learners in community with other educators. Teacher leaders share expertise, deprivatize their practice, and seek collective commitment among other educators to promote collective efficacy. A teacher who has a growth mindset about their work doesn't dwell on mistakes or an inability to reach all learners or fellow teachers—these mistakes provide growth opportunities through which they can learn. Reflection and action are part of the solution. In this sense, the more we reflect on, learn about, and improve our teaching praxis and teacher leadership actions for the betterment of student learning, the more we approach our own teacher learning with a growth mindset.

Teacher Mindset About Leadership

A teacher leadership growth mindset means that you have a growth mindset in the leadership domain. And like mindsets in any domain, beliefs about yourself affect motivation and persistence. Similarly, development of a leadership growth mindset includes understanding that our minds are malleable, that skills and knowledge make us more confident, and that challenges are opportunities for growth.

Teacher leadership is complex because the nonpositional nature of most teacher leaders and the egalitarian nature of the teacher's world are often combined with environmental mindsets that hierarchical leaders are the sole leaders in schools. Yes, teacher leadership is multifaceted, and this leadership acts in positional, hybrid, and informal roles. Looking at the unlimited possibilities of teacher leadership, there is power in recognizing and supporting teacher leadership for the vast number of teachers who are informally leading. Great things can happen when we invite and nurture teacher leadership! We know that teacher leaders are agents of change who lead without being given formal authority. Instead, their authority comes from the deep knowledge base, relationship base, and vision base that teacher leaders emerge from.

Teacher leaders work on the ground floor of educational change. This is where change is felt and seen by other teachers. The presence of collegial discourse, good working relationships, shared vision, and collaboration allows change to happen. However, change can be challenging to manage. It is not uncommon for teacher leaders who work outside the four walls of their classroom to retreat back to their rooms when the change they visualize is too slow or too hard to enable because of the status quo. This is where teacher leaders' work on sustaining and nurturing a growth mindset helps. A growth mindset sees these challenges as opportunities and links the resilience these teachers have with their persistence to be agents of change.

Reflect on your experiences as a teacher leader.

What challenges have you had as a teacher leader? How did you address those challanges? Were you able to develop additional leadership skills?

_____
_____
_____
_____
_____

How do you fill your cup up when you feel stretched? Do you circle back to what you learned in a situation and make a plan of action to persist as a teacher leader?

_____
_____
_____
_____
_____
_____

What are the mindset messages that you give yourself?

_____
_____
_____
_____
_____
_____

Leadership, along with growth and fixed mindsets, have been explored in ample research (Caniëls et al., 2018; Chase, 2010; Gottfredson & Reina, 2021). It has been found that supporting a growth mindset is a contributing factor in leadership development. To understand your own teacher leadership mindset, you must have a process of stepping outside the collective work you do as a teacher leader to monitor and self-assess your leadership growth.

Teacher leaders are not leading from above—they are leading from among. This kind of leadership entails having a deep and comprehensive understanding of teaching, working within the cultures and contexts of their schools, and leading alongside fellow teacher leaders while inviting teacher leadership as they work. It entails a growth mindset about themselves and about their job. This is a dual-growth mindset that results in happiness when both the teacher and the role (informal or formal) are in sync (Berg et al., 2023). By embracing a growth mindset, teacher leaders are more likely to take risks, invite feedback as learning opportunities, and overcome obstacles and roadblocks in their quest for schools that work together to support the teachers and students within.

Your role as a teacher leader who embraces a growth mindset can have a ripple effect for the other teachers and students at your school site. This is leadership in action; it begets followers and invites other teachers along on the journey. Teacher leadership as a growth mindset is multifaceted. The positive, supportive work that teacher leaders provide other educational stakeholders means that teacher leaders themselves are focused on positivity. This is tricky because working among loved colleagues while asking for change can be a tightrope walk, particularly in conversations among teachers when hard questions aren't typically asked.

Develop a Growth Mindset

Paying attention to our leadership path and believing that learning about leadership helps us grow are just as important as fostering a growth mindset with our students. Our leadership abilities and skills can be developed. We discussed developing teacher leader competencies in chapter 3 (page 51). And we introduced ways to co-lead among peers in chapter 4 (page 79). We also talked about being healthy in chapter 5 (page 95) because it supports leadership work. Now, let's look at some practical ways to attend to a growth mindset as teacher leaders.

Do you have a growth or fixed mindset in your approach to teacher leadership actions? Read the following sample statements and think about your actions as a teacher leader. This includes your work leading in the classroom and among your colleagues. Put a *G* next to the ones that reflect a growth mindset and an *F* next to the ones that reflect a fixed mindset.

_____ Making mistakes means I keep trying again because there is something I can learn from the experience.

_____ I'll never be a leader; leadership is what principals do.

_____ I don't need to be perfect; I just need to try. It's OK to be messy because it's a learning opportunity.

_____ That looks way too hard. I am already working hard enough. Why should I try harder?

_____ The more I practice my interpersonal and leadership skills, the better I get.

_____ I can always improve as a teacher leader.

_____ If I mess up, it's too embarrassing, and I don't like to make myself vulnerable.

Being aware of our mindset helps us grow, particularly in teacher leadership. It is a mainly self-authoring form of leadership. For most teachers, no one taps you on the shoulder and says, "you are a leader, help others in this capacity." You have to step it up yourself, weather setbacks, and pursue the teacher leadership mindset, knowing that teachers are the most valuable source to lead.

Here are some examples of growth mindset thoughts about your actions.

- **Become a lifelong learner:** Never stop growing. Keep looking for new ideas, methods, and ways of thinking about how to reach all learners. You might try studying along with your students or fellow teachers. Share what you are learning. Stay hungry for knowledge! It widens the lens.

- **Try new things:** Experiment and innovate. Maybe try lesson study or get people on board to try a new mathematics approach with you. As leaders, the more we work together, the more opportunities we have to critically reflect on practice.

- **Ask questions:** Do not be timid and think people will see you as inferior because you have a question. Are you nervous about being called out at a staff meeting? These are symptoms of a fixed mindset. Approach new ideas through an inquiry lens.

- **Let go and be flexible:** Stretch to new ideas. Keep in mind that 21st century skills are not just for students. Be open, adaptable, and learn the importance of collaboration with colleagues. It is important to stretch your boundaries to embrace multiple perspectives.

- **Be a good listener:** How often do you really listen to your colleagues? Are you trying to get your point of view across? You can open your mind to new ideas by creating a community of colleagues who truly feel heard and understood. The more we listen and collaborate, the more we grow as teacher leaders.

- **Find your support system:** Surround yourself with people who also have a leadership growth mindset and who will listen to you too. Find your allies to support you and question you on your path. This is important because you may have peers who say "we've always done it this way." They may not be supportive. Progress is not possible within their fixed mindset framework, so you need to seek out others who have a growth mindset and can support you.

- **Be mindful of praise:** Praise effort and process over results, such as saying, "Wow! That is impressive! Your hard work has paid off." You could also say something like, "Tell me about the steps you took and the process you used to get that answer."

- **Press the pause button to reflect:** To grow as a teacher leader, we need to pause and evaluate our work and outcomes. Self-reflection is a necessary part of our growth. It is important to examine our strengths and weaknesses frequently, make adjustments, and ensure that we are on track for success.

The following sections explore three major practices for supporting and building a growth mindset as a teacher leader.

Be Curious

Cultivating a sense of curiosity, love, and joy for learning helps a growth mindset. What does this mean for teacher leaders? It means you need to embrace new challenges and seek out new experiences by being open to innovation, new ideas, and perspectives. By embracing challenges as growth opportunities and valuing the learning process and the pure joy of learning, educators can develop the resilience and mindset needed to succeed in the classroom and beyond.

Teachers who demonstrate a growth mindset tend to approach learning with an emphasis on challenge and effort. As Dweck (2015) suggests, effort is important, but the strength of the growth mindset is that we learn there are different ways to approach a problem. This is important because teacher leadership is about adult learning, and we all approach learning from our own perspectives. Flexibility is key to building learning opportunities in our schools, but also how we enact teacher leadership. It includes different points of view.

Practice Gratitude and Optimism

Another important facet of developing a growth mindset is to practice gratitude and model that for others—for your colleagues, as well as your students. This involves shifting your focus to the positive things in your life and finding joy in your work.

You can do this by keeping a gratitude journal or a grateful box in your workspace. You will either write in your journal three things you are thankful for daily or write those grateful goodies on three slips of paper—folded up and tucked away in the grateful box. Then, when you are starting to feel down and negativity is creeping into your mind, glance at your journal or grateful box and read at least three entries to boost your spirits. By intentionally focusing on what we are grateful for, we reframe our experiences to seek out the positives in our lives. Remind yourself and others about making a positive difference!

Another way to share gratitude and a growth mindset is to express it openly to others. Gratitude, validated and appreciated, increases our own happiness and the well-being others feel. Express your gratitude to others; thank them for something positive they did or said. Additionally, another way to practice gratitude is to pause a few moments each day to reflect on the good things in our lives—a beautiful sunrise, a good book, or kind words from a friend.

Nurturing optimism is a direct result of having a growth mindset. Optimism is the belief that things will work out in the end and that positive outcomes are possible. We have the power within us to control our attitude every day. This is a critical step in recovering from burnout. With a growth mindset, you can view your work as an educational leader with renewed energy and enthusiasm.

Why not boost your optimism by setting realistic, doable goals? Accomplish smaller goals one step at a time and celebrate even small successes. This can help you feel motivated even when facing obstacles and challenges in the workplace. Don't forget to surround yourself with positive people who share your vision of optimism. These are colleagues who boost your spirits and inspire you.

Persevere With Grit

One way to demonstrate that you have a growth mindset is through grit. A teacher leader who has grit perseveres toward a long-term goal. They may face setbacks or challenges along the way, but with a growth mindset, they continue to move forward despite them (Duckworth, Peterson, Matthews, & Kelly, 2007). This is a matter of putting your priorities into perspective. The word *grit* suggests persistence and determination. That's what it takes for teacher leaders to model grit for their colleagues when they encounter challenging scenarios. Grit is a critical 21st century skill for all of us to develop and teach our students (Miller, 2015). Teacher leaders need to value the journey of learning because it can be supported by others or challenged.

When we persevere, we need to celebrate our successes each step of the way, so we experience progress. We often don't take time to celebrate the challenging work we have completed (or help our students celebrate). Now is the time to celebrate successes with our colleagues! Recognizing and celebrating teacher leadership is important to sustaining it. This can be challenging, as it bumps into the status quo that teacher leadership is only for the chosen few. To create a thriving culture of grit in the classroom, school, and in teacher leadership, it is important to find a balance of challenge, reflection, and authenticity. Don't forget to pause for these successes and point them out to students along the way (Heggart, 2015).

Conclusion

Teacher leadership embraces a growth mindset. Do you have one? How do you feel about being a teacher leader? Furthermore, we know that this leadership mindset is related to students' growth mindsets (Correia-Harker & Satterwhite, 2023). It is time to dig a little deeper and explore the many facets of teacher empowerment and efficacy. Developing teacher leadership will take time; it is ongoing and can be a circuitous path depending on school culture and administrative support, but schools will benefit from teacher leadership and the increased sense of community and collaboration. Teacher leadership is essential to the success of a school—yet, it can remain underutilized. It is time to reimagine teacher leadership and build it among all teacher leaders, whether their leadership is role bound or in classrooms. Teacher leaders are purpose-filled educators who seek to promote students' and each other's learning and success.

Successful teaching leadership doesn't just happen. Effective skills can be cultivated that enable teacher leaders to lead and invite others into the collective leadership work. Teacher leaders demonstrate a growth mindset as they engage in complex collegial inquiries with other educators, problem solve with colleagues, and try again to build teacher leader capacity in schools when school culture pushes back. All teachers can be leaders; it is a matter of learning about leadership, growing the skills, and maintaining a growth mindset about teacher leadership.

Epilogue

Some people believe that leadership falls into the elusive category of things that cannot be defined but are easy to identify, and that teacher leadership is even harder to categorize. We respectfully disagree. We believe that by identifying the six key components that support and develop teacher leadership, all teachers can, and must, be leaders for our students, schools, and democracy to thrive. Further, leadership does not simply happen. It requires continual effort, reflection, collaboration, and growth. In that regard, our leadership is always growing, and the six practices identified in this book are meant to guide teacher leaders on their journey.

We have asked you to consider your purpose as an educator and how that purpose has evolved from the beginning of your career to now. We have stressed the importance of continually reflecting and revisiting why you teach. While there may be similarities in the motivations that drive each educator, we firmly believe that sharing these individual motivations with colleagues creates a synergy among peers and enables an environment that is open to growth.

Every teacher has tools available to grow their leadership practice once they realize that they don't need permission to lead. Teachers can draw on external tools and frameworks, but there are also internal tools that every teacher can access. Our hope is that they can recognize that leadership abounds in the profession and there is an open invitation to join the party. While many believe that the flat, egalitarian nature of a school results in a hierarchical leadership structure, our goal has been to illustrate the many ways that teachers can widen their viewpoint and understand that leadership is within their grasp, whether formalized with a positional title or by rising organically among a group of like-minded educators.

How often have you heard that change is the only constant? The world of education is constantly changing, and teachers can lead the charge. To do so, they must hone their individual teacher efficacy and recognize that by linking their efficacy with that of their fellow teachers they create a collective efficacy that is truly greater than the sum of the parts. By harnessing this collective efficacy, teachers can be the agents of change that will propel our students and schools forward. The good news is that there are a plethora of tools available to help teachers grow through formalized professional development or teacher-driven collaborative work.

The glue that holds collaborative efforts together is the strength of the relationships that teachers develop with each other. Good relationships depend on a high level of emotional intelligence so that colleagues can hold free and frank conversations that encourage honest discourse and are devoid of defensive posturing and closed minds.

Anybody in the teaching profession knows that teaching is hard but important work, and layering in teacher leadership adds another level of complexity to an already demanding calling. We acknowledge that the journey to leadership requires effort, and the reward is that we collectively create schools where all students learn and thrive as members of our school communities. This important work is ongoing. Know that we support you in this work and that we see your efforts.

References and Resources

Aguilar, E. (2018). *Onward: Cultivating emotional resilience in educators.* San Francisco: Jossey-Bass.

Ainsworth, S., & Oldfield, J. (2019). Quantifying teacher resilience: Context matters. *Teaching and Teacher Education, 82,* 117–128.

Andrei, E., Ellerbe, M., & Cherner, T. (2015). "The text opened my eyes": A book club on teaching writing to ELLs. *TESL–EJ, 19*(3), 1–22.

Angelle, P. S., & Beaumont, J. (2006). Teacher leadership: A definitional perspective from principals and teachers. In Annual Meeting of the University Council for Educational Administration.

Angelle, P. S., & DeHart, C. A. (2011). Teacher perceptions of teacher leadership: Examining differences by experience, degree, and position. *NASSP Bulletin, 95*(2), 141–160. Accessed at https://citeseerx.ist.psu.edu/document?repid=rep1&type=pdf&doi=7f68cb4ae483e34957f061620dfd166c99ff7415 on February 19, 2024.

Avgitidou, S. (2020). Facilitating teachers as action researchers and reflective practitioners: New issues and proposals. *Educational Action Research, 28*(2), 175–191.

Baloche, L. (2014). Everybody has a story: Storytelling as a community building exploration of equity and access. *Intercultural Education, 25*(3), 206–215.

Bambino, D. (2002). Critical friends. *Educational Leadership, 59*(6), 25–27.

Bandura, A. (1997). *Self-efficacy: The exercise of control.* New York: W. H. Freeman.

Barbor, C. (2001, May 1). The science of meditation. *Psychology Today.* Accessed at www.psychologytoday.com/us/articles/200105/the-science-meditation on February 19, 2024.

Barrenechea, I. (2022). Teachers' perceived sense of well-being through the lens of mattering: Reclaiming the sense of community. *Journal of Professional Capital and Community, 7*(4), 369–389.

Barth, R. S. (2006). Improving relationships within the schoolhouse. *Educational Leadership, 63*(6), 8–13.

Beaubien, J., Stahl, L., Herter, R., & Paunesku, D. (2016, February). *Promoting learning mindsets in schools: Lessons from educators' engagement with the PERTS mindset kit.* Stanford, CA: Project for Education Research That Scales. Accessed at https://p3.perts.net/static/documents/Mindset_Kit_Engagement_Report.pdf on February 19, 2024.

Beauchamp, C. (2015). Reflection in teacher education: Issues emerging from a review of current literature. *Reflective Practice, 16*(1), 123–141.

Beauchamp, C., & Thomas, L. (2010). Reflecting on an ideal: Student teachers envision a future identity. *Reflective Practice, 11*(5), 631–643.

Beijaard, D., & Meijer, P. C. (2017). Developing the personal and professional in making a teacher identity. *The SAGE Handbook of Research on Teacher Education, 2,* 177–192.

Benson-O'Connor, C., Carr, J., Farrar, L., LeMasters, J., McDaniel, C. L., & Hunzicker, J. (2020). Action research in STEM: Teacher-led projects from primary to middle school. *School–University Partnerships, 12*(4), 142–152.

Berg, J. H., Carver, C. L., & Mangin, M. M. (2014). Teacher leader model standards: Implications for preparation, policy, and practice. *Journal of Research on Leadership Education, 9*(2), 195–217.

Berg, J. M., Wrzesniewski, A., Grant, A. M., Kurkoski, J., & Welle, B. (2023). Getting unstuck: The effects of growth mindsets about the self and job on happiness at work. *Journal of Applied Psychology, 108*(1), 152–166.

Bergmark, U., Lundström, S., Manderstedt, L., & Palo, A. (2018). Why become a teacher? Student teachers' perceptions of the teaching profession and motives for career choice. *European Journal of Teacher Education, 41*(3), 266–281.

Berry, B., Daughtrey, A., & Wieder, A. (2010, January). *Teacher leadership: Leading the way to effective teaching and learning.* Washington, DC: Center for Teaching Quality. Accessed at https://files.eric.ed.gov/fulltext/ED509719.pdf on March 4, 2024.

Bigham, E., McDannel, L., Luciano, I., & Salgado-Lopez, G. (2014). Effect of a brief guided imagery on stress. *Biofeedback (Online), 42*(1), 28–35.

Bintz, W. P., & Dillard, J. (2007). Teachers as reflective practitioners: Examining teacher stories of curricular change in a 4th grade classroom. *Reading Horizons: A Journal of Literacy and Language Arts, 47*(3), 203–228.

Bissessar, C. S. (2014). An exploration of the relationship between teachers' psychological capital and their collective self-esteem. *Australian Journal of Teacher Education (Online), 39*(9), 35–52.

Blake, J., & Gibson, A. (2021). Critical friends group protocols deepen conversations in collaborative action research projects. *Educational Action Research, 29*(1), 133–148.

Blanton, B. S., Broemmel, A. D., & Rigell, A. (2020). Speaking volumes: Professional development through book studies. *American Educational Research Journal, 57*(3), 1014–1044.

Boaler, J. (2016). *Mistakes grow your brain*. YouCubed. Stanford University. Graduate School of Education.

Boaler, J. (2019). *Limitless mind: Learn, lead, and live without barriers*. New York: HarperOne.

Bond, N. (2021). Teacher leadership in an elementary school: A case study of instructional support specialists. *Education, 141*(4), 201–213.

Brainwaves Video Anthology. (2014, April 29). *Andy Hargreaves—Professional capital: Transforming teaching in every school* [Video file]. Accessed at www.youtube.com/watch?v=w7LQhLX2Wek on October 26, 2023.

Brassell, D. (2011). *Bringing joy back into the classroom*. Huntington Beach, CA: Shell Education.

Brown, B. (2010). *The gifts of imperfection: Let go of who you think you're supposed to be and embrace who you are*. Center City, MN: Hazelden.

Brown, B. (2021). *Atlas of the heart: Mapping meaningful connection and the language of human experience*. New York: Random House.

Buchanan, R. (2015). Teacher identity and agency in an era of accountability. *Teachers and Teaching: Theory and Practice, 21*(6), 700–719.

Buchanan, R., Mills, T., Edward, B., Mathieu, E., Snyder, M., & Weitman, M., et al. (2023). Teacher leadership collaborative: Boundary-crossing spaces for teacher empowerment. *Professional Development in Education, 49*(6), 1152–1166.

Bui, P., Pongsakdi, N., McMullen, J., Lehtinen, E., & Hannula-Sormunen, M. M. (2023). A systematic review of mindset interventions in mathematics classrooms: What works and what does not? *Educational Research Review, 40*, Article 100554.

Caniëls, M. C. J., Semeijn, J. H., & Renders, I. H. M. (2018). Mind the mindset! The interaction of proactive personality, transformational leadership and growth mindset for engagement at work. *Career Development International, 23*(1), 48–66.

Commission on Teacher Credentialing. (2009). *California standards for the teaching profession.* Sacramento, CA: Author. Accessed at www.ctc.ca.gov/docs/default-source/educator-prep/standards/cstp-2009.pdf?sfvrsn=c9747b7e_2 on February 19, 2024.

Carswell, M. A. (2021). Developing the leadership capacity of teachers: Theory to practice. *Journal of School Administration Research and Development, 6*(1), 52–59.

Cashman, K. (2008). *Leadership from the inside out: Becoming a leader for life* (2nd ed.). San Francisco: Berrett-Koehler.

Chang, M.-L. (2009). An appraisal perspective of teacher burnout: Examining the emotional work of teachers. *Educational Psychology Review, 21*(3), 193–218.

Chang-Kredl, S., & Kingsley, S. (2014). Identity expectations in early childhood teacher education: Pre-service teachers' memories of prior experiences and reasons for entry into the profession. *Teaching and Teacher Education, 43,* 27–36. https://doi.org/10.1016/j.tate.2014.05.005

Chase, M. A. (2010). Should coaches believe in innate ability? The importance of leadership mindset. *Quest, 62*(3), 296–307.

Chen, Y.-C., Wu, H.-K., & Hsin, C.-T. (2022). Science teaching in kindergartens: Factors associated with teachers' self-efficacy and outcome expectations for integrating science into teaching. *International Journal of Science Education, 44*(7), 1045–1066.

Cherkowski, S. (2018). Positive teacher leadership: Building mindsets and capacities to grow wellbeing. *International Journal of Teacher Leadership, 9*(1), 63–78.

Chiappetta, E. (2023, February 1). *A protocol for teacher-focused PD.* Accessed at www.edutopia.org/article/critical-friends-group-protocol-pd/ on October 27, 2023.

Chiong, C., Menzies, L., & Parameshwaran, M. (2017). Why do long-serving teachers stay in the teaching profession? Analysing the motivations of teachers with 10 or more years' experience in England. *British Educational Research Journal, 43*(6), 1083–1110.

Clandinin, D. J., Downey, C. A, & Huber, J. (2009). Attending to changing landscapes: Shaping the interwoven identities of teachers and teacher educators. *Asia-Pacific Journal of Teacher Education, 37*(2), 141–154.

Cochran-Smith, M., & Lytle, S. L. (2009). *Inquiry as stance: Practitioner research for the next generation.* New York: Teachers College Press.

Cochran-Smith, M., McQuillan, P., Mitchell, K., Terrell, D. G., Barnatt, J., & D'Souza, L., et al. (2012). A longitudinal study of teaching practice and early career decisions: A cautionary tale. *American Educational Research Journal, 49*(5), 844–880.

Collie, R. J., & Perry, N. E. (2019). Cultivating teacher thriving through social–emotional competence and its development. *The Australian Educational Researcher, 46*(4), 699–714.

Collins, J. (2001). *Good to great: Why some companies make the leap. . . and others don't.* New York: HarperCollins.

Collinson, V. (2012). Leading by learning, learning by leading. *Professional Development in Education, 38*(2), 247–266.

Correia-Harker, B. P., & Satterwhite, R. (2023). Leadership learning. In S. R. Komives & J. E. Owen (Eds.), *A Research Agenda for Leadership Learning and Development through Higher Education*. Northampton, MA: Edward Elgar.

Coughlan, M. (2015). *Teacher leadership: Connecting learning to practice* [Doctoral dissertation, Saint Mary's College of California]. ProQuest. www.proquest.com/docview/1765385634

Crowther, F., Ferguson, M., & Hann, L. (2009). *Developing teacher leaders: How teacher leadership enhances school success*. Thousand Oaks, CA: Corwin Press.

Czubaj, C. (1996). Maintaining teacher motivation. *Education, 116*(3), 372–378.

Danielson, C. (2006). *Teacher leadership that strengthens professional practice*. Alexandria, VA: ASCD.

Darling-Hammond, L. (1996). What matters most: A competent teacher for every child. *Phi Delta Kappan, 78*(3), 193–200.

Davis, M., Eshelman, E. R., & McKay, M. (2008). *The relaxation and stress reduction workbook*. Oakland, CA: New Harbinger Publications.

Day, C., Kington, A., Stobart, G., & Sammons, P. (2006). The personal and professional selves of teachers: Stable and unstable identities. *British Educational Research Journal, 32*(4), 601–616.

Day, C., Sammons, P., Stobart, G., Kington, A., & Gu, Q. (2007). *Teachers matter: Connecting work, lives and effectiveness*. New York: Open University Press.

Degol, J. L., Wang, M.-T., Zhang, Y., & Allerton, J. (2018). Do growth mindsets in math benefit females? Identifying pathways between gender, mindset, and motivation. *Journal of Youth and Adolescence, 47*, 976–990.

DeLuca, C., Shulha, J., Luhanga, U., Shulha, L. M., Christou, T. M., & Klinger, D. A. (2014). Collaborative inquiry as a professional learning structure for educators: A scoping review. *Professional Development in Education, 41*(4), 640–670.

Dhingra, N., Samo, A., Schaninger, B., & Schrimper, M. (2021, April 5). *Help your employees find purpose—or watch them leave*. McKinsey & Company. Accessed at www.mckinsey.com/capabilities/people-and-organizational-performance/our-insights/help-your-employees-find-purpose-or-watch-them-leave on February 19, 2024.

Doherty, J. (2020). A systematic review of literature on teacher attrition and school-related factors that affect it. *Teacher Education Advancement Network Journal, 12*(1), 75–85.

Donohoo, J., Hattie, J., & Eells, R. (2018, March). The power of collective efficacy. *Educational Leadership*, *75*(6), 40–44.

Donohoo, J., & Velasco, M. (2016). *The transformative power of collaborative inquiry: Realizing change in schools and classrooms*. Thousand Oaks, CA: Corwin Press.

Drago-Severson, E. (2009). *Leading adult learning: Supporting adult development in our schools*. Thousand Oaks, CA: Corwin Press.

Duckworth, A. L., Peterson, C., Matthews, M. D., & Kelly, D. R. (2007). Grit: Perseverance and passion for long-term goals. *Journal of Personality and Social Psychology*, *92*(6), 1087–1101.

DuFour, R., DuFour, R., Eaker, R., & Many, T. (2010). *Learning by doing: A handbook for Professional Learning Communities at Work* (2nd ed.). Bloomington, IN: Solution Tree Press.

DuFour, R., DuFour, R., Eaker, R., Many, T. W., & Mattos, M. (2016). *Learning by doing: A handbook for Professional Learning Communities at Work* (3rd ed.). Bloomington, IN: Solution Tree Press.

DuFour, R., Eaker, R., & DuFour, R. (Eds.). (2005). *On common ground: The power of Professional Learning Communities*. Bloomington, IN: Solution Tree Press.

Dweck, C. S. (2007). *Mindset: The new psychology of success* (Updated ed.). New York: Ballentine.

Dweck, C. S. (2009). Mindsets: Developing talent through a growth mindset. *Olympic Coach*, *21*(1), 4–7.

Dweck, C. S. (2015, September 22). Carol Dweck revisits the "growth mindset." *Education Week*, *35*(5), 20–24.

Dweck, C. S., Chiu, C., and Hong, Y. (1995). Implicit theories and their role in judgements and reactions: A world from two perspectives. *Psychological Inquiry*, *6*(4), 267–285.

Dweck, C. S., & Yeager, D. S. (2019). Mindsets: A view from two eras. *Perspectives on Psychological Science*, *14*(3), 481–496.

Edenfield, T. M., & Blumenthal, J. A. (2011). Exercise and stress reduction. In R. J. Contrada & A. Baum (Eds.), *The handbook of stress science: Biology, psychology, and health* (pp. 301–319). New York: Springer.

Elster, M. J., O'Sullivan, P. S., Muller-Juge, V., Sheu, L., Kaiser, S. V., & Hauer, K. E. (2022). Does being a coach benefit clinician-educators? A mixed methods study of faculty self-efficacy, job satisfaction and burnout. *Perspectives on Medical Education*, *11*(1), 45–52.

Esparza, J., Shumow, L., & Schmidt, J. A. (2014). Growth mindset of gifted seventh grade students in science. *NCSSSMST Journal, 19*(1), 6–13.

Fairman, J. C., & Mackenzie, S. V. (2012). Spheres of teacher leadership action for learning. *Professional Development in Education, 38*(2), 229–246.

Fairman, J. C., & Mackenzie, S. V. (2015). How teacher leaders influence others and understand their leadership. *International Journal of Leadership in Education, 18*(1), 61–87.

Farmer, D. (2020). Teacher attrition: The impacts of stress. *Delta Kappa Gamma Bulletin, 87*(1), 41–50.

Feiman-Nemser, S. (2012, May). Beyond solo teaching. *Educational Leadership, 69*(8), 10–16.

Firestone, W. A., & Martinez, M. C. (2007). Districts, teacher leaders, and distributed leadership: Changing instructional practice. *Leadership and Policy in Schools, 6*(1), 3–35.

Flores, M. A., & Day, C. (2006). Contexts which shape and reshape new teachers' identities: A multi-perspective study. *Teaching and Teacher Education, 22*(2), 219–232.

Frondozo, C. E., King, R. B., Nalipay, M. J. N., & Mordeno, I. G. (2022). Mindsets matter for teachers, too: Growth mindset about teaching ability predicts teachers' enjoyment and engagement. *Current Psychology, 41*(8), 5030–5033.

Fujii, T. (2016). Designing and adapting tasks in lesson planning: A critical process of lesson study. *ZDM: The International Journal on Mathematics Education, 48*(4), 411–423.

Fullan, M., Quinn, J., & McEachen, J. (2017). *Deep learning: Engage the world change the world*. Thousand Oaks, CA: Corwin Press.

Galloway, C. M. (1976). Interpersonal relations and education. *Theory Into Practice, 15*(5), 316–318.

Gaudreault, K. L., Richards, K. A. R., & Woods, A. M. (2018). Understanding the perceived mattering of physical education teachers. *Sport, Education and Society, 23*(6), 578–590.

Ghanizadeh, A., & Jahedizadeh, S. (2015). Teacher burnout: A review of sources and ramifications. *British Journal of Education, Society and Behavioural Science, 6*(1), 24–39.

Gilles, C., Davis, B., & McGlamery, S. (2009). Induction programs that work. *Phi Delta Kappan, 91*(2), 42–47.

Glanz, J. (2003). *Action research: An educational leader's guide to school improvement* (2nd ed.). Lanham, MD: Rowman & Littlefield.

Goddard, R. D., Hoy, W. K., & Hoy, A. W. (2000). Collective teacher efficacy: Its meaning, measure, and impact on student achievement. *American Educational Research Journal, 37*(2), 479–507.

Goleman, D. (2005). *Emotional intelligence: Why it can matter more than IQ* (10th anniversary edition). New York: Random House.

Goleman, D. (2011). *Leadership: The power of emotional intelligence.* Northampton, MA: More Than Sound.

Goleman, D. (2019). *The emotionally intelligent leader.* Brighton, MA: Harvard Business Review Press.

Goleman, D., McKee, A., & Achor, S. (2017). *Everyday emotional intelligence: Big ideas and practical advice on how to be human at work.* Brighton, MA: Harvard Business Review Press.

Goodwin, B., & Shebby, S. (2020). Restoring teachers' efficacy. *Educational Leadership, 78*(4), 76–77.

Gordon, L. M. (2012, June 6). *Good teaching matters, teachers matter, and teacher education matters* [Keynote address]. Student Teaching Reception, Occidental College, Los Angeles, CA.

Gordon, S. P., Jacobs, J., Croteau, S. M., & Solis, R. (2021). Informal teacher leaders: Who they are, what they do, and how they impact teaching and learning. *Journal of School Leadership, 31*(6), 526–547. https://doi.org/10.1177/1052684620924468

Gottfredson, R. K., & Reina, C. S. (2021). Illuminating the foundational role that mindsets should play in leadership development. *Business Horizons, 64*(4), 439–451.

Gould-Yakovleva, O., McVee, M., & Fronczak, D. (2020). "Ready-Ready" to teach: The telling case of a reflective teacher-practitioner. *The Qualitative Report, 25*(2), 306–319.

Gregory, J. L. (2017). Trust relationships in schools: Supporting or subverting implementation of school-wide initiatives. *School Leadership and Management, 37*(1–2), 141–161.

Gu, Q., & Day, C. (2007). Teachers resilience: A necessary condition for effectiveness. *Teaching and Teacher Education, 23*(8), 1302–1316.

Gul, T., Demir, K., & Criswell, B. (2019). Constructing teacher leadership through mentoring: Functionality of mentoring practices in evolving teacher leadership. *Journal of Science Teacher Education, 30*(3), 209–228.

Gunn, J. (2018). *Building a growth mindset for teachers.* Accessed at https://resilient educator.com/classroom-resources/growth-mindset-for-teachers/ on February 20, 2024.

Hammerness, K. (2008). "If you don't know where you are going, any path will do": The role of teachers' visions in teachers' career paths. *The New Educator, 4*(1), 1–22.

Hargreaves, A., & Shirley, D. L. (2012). *The global fourth way: The quest for educational excellence.* Thousand Oaks, CA: Corwin Press.

Harris, S., Lowery-Moore, H., & Farrow, V. (2008). Extending transfer of learning theory to transformative learning theory: A model for promoting teacher leadership. *Theory Into Practice, 47*(4), 318–326.

Harrison, C., & Killion, J. (2007). Ten roles for teacher leaders. *Educational Leadership, 65*(1), 74–77.

Hascher, T., Beltman, S., & Mansfield, C. (2021). Teacher wellbeing and resilience: Towards an integrative model. *Educational Research, 63*(4), 416–439.

Hattie, J. (2015). The applicability of Visible Learning to higher education. *Scholarship of Teaching and Learning in Psychology, 1*(1), 79–91.

Hattie, J. (2023). *Visible learning: The sequel: A synthesis of over 2,100 meta-analyses relating to achievement.* New York: Routledge.

Heggart, K. (2015). *Developing a growth mindset in teachers and staff.* Accessed at www.edutopia.org/discussion/developing-growth-mindset-teachers-and-staff on February 20, 2024.

Heinz, M. (2015). Why choose teaching? An international review of empirical studies exploring student teachers' career motivations and levels of commitment to teaching. *Educational Research and Evaluation, 21*(3), 258–297.

Hickey, W. D., & Harris, S. (2005). Improved professional development through teacher leadership. *The Rural Educator, 26*(2), 12–16.

Hoerr, T. R. (2013). *Fostering grit: How do I prepare my students for the real world?* Alexandria, VA: ASCD.

Hord, S. M., & Sommers, W. A. (2008). *Leading professional learning communities: Voices from research and practice.* Thousand Oaks, CA: Corwin Press.

Horvath, M., Goodell, J. E., & Kosteas, V. D. (2018). Decisions to enter and continue in the teaching profession: Evidence from a sample of U.S. secondary STEM teacher candidates. *Teaching and Teacher Education, 71*, 57–65.

Howe, E. R. (2006). Exemplary teacher induction: An international review. *Educational Philosophy and Theory, 38*(3), 287–297.

Huggins, K. S., Lesseig, K., & Rhodes, H. (2017). Rethinking teacher leader development: A study of early career mathematics teachers. *International Journal of Teacher Leadership, 8*(2), 28–48.

Hunzicker, J. (2014). The path to teacher leadership. *AMLE Magazine, 2*(2), 10–13.

Hunzicker, J. (2018). Teacher leadership in professional development schools: A definition, brief history, and call for further study. In J. Hunzicker (Ed.), *Teacher leadership in professional development schools* (pp. 19–37). Leeds, England: Emerald.

Hunzicker, J. (2020). The impact of teacher leadership on student learning in professional development schools (PDS): Action research is important. *School–University Partnerships, 12*(4), 1–9.

Jacobs, R. (2017). *The 7 questions to find your purpose.* London: Watkins.

Johannesson, P. (2022). Development of professional learning communities through action research: understanding professional learning in practice. *Educational Action Research, 30*(3), 411–426.

Johnson, E. S. (2020). *Action research.* Oxford Research Encyclopedia of Education. Accessed at https://oxfordre.com/education/display/10.1093/acrefore/9780190264093.001.0001/acrefore-9780190264093-e-696 on February 20, 2024.

Johnston, I. (2017). Creating a growth mindset. *Strategic HR Review, 16*(4), 155–160.

Jonsson, A.-C., Beach, D., Korp, H., & Erlandson, P. (2012). Teachers' implicit theories of intelligence: Influences from different disciplines and scientific theories. *European Journal of Teacher Education, 35*(4), 387–400.

Katzenmeyer, M., & Moller, G. (2009). *Awakening the sleeping giant: Helping teachers develop as leaders* (3rd ed.). Thousand Oaks, CA: Corwin Press.

Keiler, L. S. (2018). Teachers' roles and identities in student-centered classrooms. *International Journal of STEM Education, 5*(1), 1–20.

Kelchtermans, G. (2009). Who I am in how I teach is the message: Self-understanding, vulnerability, and reflection. *Teachers and Teaching: Theory and Practice, 15*(2), 257–272.

Killion, J., & Harrison, C. (2017). *Taking the lead: New roles for teachers and school-based coaches* (2nd ed.). Oxford, OH: Learning Forward.

King, B., & Smith, C. (2020). Using project-based learning to develop teachers for leadership. *The Clearing House: A Journal of Educational Strategies, Issues and Ideas, 93*(3), 158–164.

Klassen, R. M., & Tze, V. M. C. (2014). Teachers' self-efficacy, personality, and teaching effectiveness: A meta-analysis. *Educational Research Review, 12*, 59–76.

Kouzes, T. K., & Posner, B. Z. (2019). Influence of managers' mindset on leadership behavior. *Leadership and Organization Development Journal, 40*(8), 829–844.

Kovacs, L., & Corrie, S. (2017). Building reflective capability to enhance coaching practice. *The Coaching Psychologist, 13*(1), 4–12.

Kwok, A., Rios, A., & Kwok, M. (2022). Pre-service teachers' motivations to enter the profession. *Journal of Curriculum Studies, 54*(4), 576–597.

Lai, E., & Cheung, D. (2015). Enacting teacher leadership: The role of teachers in bringing about change. Educational Management, Administration & Leadership, 43(5), 673–692.

Lambert, L. (2003). *Leadership capacity for lasting school improvement.* Alexandria, VA: ASCD.

Lambert, L., Zimmerman, D. P., & Gardner, M. E. (2016). *Liberating leadership capacity: Pathways to educational wisdom.* New York: Teachers College Press.

Larrivee, B. (2008). Development of a tool to assess teachers' level of reflective practice. *Reflective Practice, 9*(3), 341–360.

Larkin, R. W. (1973). Contextual influences on teacher leadership styles. *Sociology of Education, 46*(4), 471–479.

Lassonde, C. A., & Israel, S. E. (2010). *Teacher collaboration for professional learning: Facilitating study, research, and inquiry communities.* San Francisco: Jossey-Bass.

Lawrence, D. (1999). *Teaching with confidence: A guide to enhancing teacher self-esteem.* Thousand Oaks, CA: SAGE.

Lee, J. S., Sachs, D., & Wheeler, L. (2014). The crossroads of teacher leadership and action research. *The Clearing House, 87*(5), 218–223.

Leiter, M. P., & Maslach, C. (2024). Job burnout. In handbook of occupational health psychology, 3rd ed., 291–307. American Psychological Association.

Lewin, K. (1946). Action research and minority problems. *Journal of Social Issues,* 2, 4, 34–46. Accessed at https://doi.org/10.1111/j.1540-4560.1946.tb02295.x on May 1, 2024.

Lieberman, A., Hanson, S., & Gless, J. (2012). *Mentoring teachers: Navigating the real-world tensions.* San Francisco: Jossey-Bass.

Little, J. W. (2003). Constructions of teacher leadership in three periods of policy and reform activism. *School Leadership and Management, 23*(4), 401–419.

Liu, Y., & Liao, W. (2019). Professional development and teacher efficacy: Evidence from the 2013 TALIS. *School Effectiveness and School Improvement, 30*(4), 487–509.

Louis, K. S., & Marks, H. M. (1998). Does professional community affect the classroom? Teachers' work and students' experiences in restructuring schools. *American Journal of Education, 106*(4), 532–575.

Lowery, K. (2019). Educators' perceptions of the value of coach mindset development for their well-being. *International Journal of Mentoring and Coaching in Education, 8*(4), 310–324.

Lukacs, K. S., & Galluzzo, G. R. (2014). Beyond empty vessels and bridges: Toward defining teachers as the agents of school change. *Teacher Development*, *18*(1), 100–106.

Lumpkin, A., Claxton, H., & Wilson, A. (2014). Key characteristics of teacher leaders in schools. *Administrative Issues Journal: Connecting Education, Practice, and Research*, *4*(2), 59–67.

Macdonald, D. (1999). Teacher attrition: A review of literature. *Teaching and Teacher Education*, *15*(8), 835–848.

Mangin, M. M. (2005). Distributed leadership and the culture of schools: Teacher leaders' strategies for gaining access to classrooms. *Journal of School Leadership*, *15*(4), 456–484.

Mangin, M. M. (2010). Building relationships step by step: One teacher leader's journey. *Journal of Cases in Educational Leadership*, *13*(2), 13–20.

Mangin, M. M., & Stoelinga, S. R. (2009). The future of instructional teacher leader roles. *Educational Forum*, *74*(1), 49–62.

Mangin, M., & Stoelinga, S. (2011). Peer? Expert? Teacher leaders struggle to gain trust while establishing their expertise. *Journal of Staff Development*, *32*(3), 48–51.

Mansfield, C., Beltman, S., Weatherby-Fell, N., & Broadley, T. (2016). Classroom ready? Building resilience in teacher education. *Teacher Education: Innovation, Intervention and Impact*, 211–229.

Manuel, J., & Hughes, J. (2006). "It has always been my dream": Exploring pre-service teachers' motivations for choosing to teach. *Teacher Development*, *10*(1), 5–24.

Margolis, J. (2012). Hybrid teacher leaders and the new professional development ecology. *Professional Development in Education*, *38*(2), 291–315.

Margolis, J. (2020). The semiformality of teacher leadership on the edge of chaos. *Harvard Educational Review*, *90*(3), 397–418.

Markkanen, P., Välimäki, M., Anttila, M., & Kuuskorpi, M. (2020). A reflective cycle: Understanding challenging situations in a school setting. *Educational Research*, *62*(1), 46–62.

Maslach, C., & Leiter, M. P. (2008). *The truth about burnout: How organizations cause personal stress and what to do about it*. San Francisco: Jossey-Bass.

Maslach, C., Schaufeli, W. B., & Leiter, M. (2001). Job burnout. *Annual Review of Psychology*, *52*, 397–422.

Mason, S., Weeden, E., & Bogaard, D. (2022, September). *Building a growth mindset toolkit as a means toward developing a growth mindset for faculty interactions with students in and out of the classroom: building a growth mindset toolkit for faculty* [Conference Presentation]. Proceedings of the 23rd Annual Conference on Information Technology Education. Chicago, IL.

Maxwell, J. C. (2007). *The 21 irrefutable laws of leadership: Follow them and people will follow you.* New York: HarperCollins Leadership.

Mesler, R. M., Corbin, C. M., & Martin, B. H. (2021). Teacher mindset is associated with development of students' growth mindset. *Journal of Applied Developmental Psychology, 76,* Article 101299.

Meyer, F., & Slater-Brown, K. (2022). Educational change doesn't come easy: lead teachers' work as change agents. *Mathematics Education Research Journal, 34*(1), 139–163.

Mezirow, J. (1991). *Transformative dimensions of adult learning.* San Francisco: Jossey-Bass.

Miller, A. K. (2015). *Freedom to fail: How do I foster risk-taking and innovation in my classroom?* Alexandria, VA: ASCD.

Miller, H. L. (2023, October 25). *15 of the world's best leadership books.* Accessed at https://leaders.com/articles/leadership/leadership-books/ on February 20, 2024.

Molden, D. C., & Dweck, C. S. (2006). Finding "meaning" in psychology: A lay theories approach to self-regulation, social perception, and social development. *American Psychologist, 61*(3), 192–203.

Moore, T. L. M. B., & Shaughnessy, M. (2012). Carol Dweck's views on achievement and intelligence: implications for education. *Research Journal in Organizational Psychology and Educational Studies, 1*(3), 174–184.

Murphy, J. (2005). *Connecting teacher leadership and school improvement.* Thousand Oaks, CA: Corwin Press.

Murphy, M. C., & Reeves, S. L. (2019). Personal and organizational mindsets at work. *Research in Organizational Behavior, 39*(2), Article 100121.

Nalipay, M. J. N., King, R. B., Mordeno, I. G., Chai, C.-S., & Jong, M. S.-Y. (2021). Teachers with a growth mindset are motivated and engaged: The relationships among mindsets, motivation, and engagement in teaching. *Social Psychology of Education, 24*(6), 1663–1684.

National Board for Professional Teaching Standards. (2024). *Standards: Written for teachers by teachers.* Arlington, VA: Author. Accessed at www.nbpts.org/certification/standards/ on February 20, 2024.

National Center for Principled Leadership & Research Ethics. (2021). *Annenberg Institute Critical Friends Consultancy Summary.* Urbana, IL: Author.

National Commission on Excellence in Education. (1983). *A nation at risk: The imperative for educational reform.* Washington, DC: Author. Accessed at https://edreform.com/wp-content/uploads/2013/02/A_Nation_At_Risk_1983.pdf on February 20, 2024.

National Education Association. (2018). *The teacher leadership competencies.* Washington, DC: Author. Accessed at www.nea.org/sites/default/files/2021-03/2019%20TLI%20Competency%20Book%20NEA_TLCF_20180824.pdf on February 20, 2024.

National Education Association. (2020, July). *The teacher leader model standards.* Washington, DC: Author. Accessed at www.nea.org/resource-library/teacher-leader-model-standards on February 20, 2024.

National Governors Association Center for Best Practices & Council of Chief State School Officers. (2010). *Common Core State Standards for English language arts and literacy in history/social studies, science, and technical subjects.* Washington, DC: Authors. Accessed at https://corestandards.org/wp-content/uploads/2023/09/ELA_Standards1.pdf on February 20, 2024.

Nelson, T. H., Deuel, A., Slavit, D., & Kennedy, A. (2010). Leading deep conversations in collaborative inquiry groups. *The Clearing House, 83*(5), 175–179.

Neumerski, C. M. (2013). Rethinking instructional leadership, a review: What do we know about principal, teacher, and coach instructional leadership, and where should we go from here? *Educational Administration Quarterly, 49*(2), 310–347.

Nguyen, D., Harris, A., & Ng, D. (2020). A review of the empirical research on teacher leadership (2003–2017): Evidence, patterns and implications. *Journal of Educational Administration, 58*(1), 60–80.

Nias, J. (1996). Thinking about feeling: The emotions in teaching. *Cambridge Journal of Education, 26*(3), 293–306.

No Child Left Behind (NCLB) Act of 2001, Pub. L. No. 107-110, § 115, Stat. 1425 (2002).

Nygaard, K. (2019). The causes of teacher burnout and attrition [Thesis, Concordia University, St. Paul]. Digital Commons. https://digitalcommons.csp.edu/teacher-education_masters/10

Olsen, B. (2008). How reasons for entry into the profession illuminate teacher identity development. *Teacher Education Quarterly, 35*(3), 23–40.

Organisation for Economic Co-operation and Development (OECD). (2018). *The future of education and skills: Education 2030.* Paris: Author. Accessed at www.oecd.org/education/2030/E2030%20Position%20Paper%20(05.04.2018).pdf on February 20, 2024.

Ostorga, A. N. (2006). Developing teachers who are reflective practitioners: A complex process. *Issues in Teacher Education, 15*(2), 5–20.

Peklaj, C. (2015). Teacher competencies through the prism of educational research. *Center for Educational Policy Studies Journal, 5*(3), 183–204.

Perciavalle, V., Blandini, M., Fecarotta, P., Buscemi, A., Di Corrado, D., & Bertolo, L., et al. (2017). The role of deep breathing on stress. *Neurological Sciences, 38*(3), 451–458.

Pierson, R. F. (2013, May). *Every kid needs a champion* [Video file]. TED Conferences. Accessed at www.ted.com/talks/rita_pierson_every_kid_needs_a_champion?language=en on October 30, 2023.

Pink, D. H. (2011). *Drive: The surprising truth about what motivates us.* New York: Riverhead Books.

Podolsky, A. K., Kini, T., & Darling-Hammond, L. (2019). Does teaching experience increase teacher effectiveness? A review of research. *Journal of Professional Capital and Community, 4*(4), 286–308.

Poekert, P. E. (2012). Teacher leadership and professional development: Examining links between two concepts central to school improvement. *Professional Development in Education, 38*(2), 169–188.

Pounder, J. S. (2006). Transformational classroom leadership: The fourth wave of teacher leadership? *Educational Management Administration and Leadership, 34*(4), 533–545.

Prenger, R., Poortman, C. L., & Handelzalts, A. (2021). Professional learning networks: From teacher learning to school improvement? *Journal of Educational Change, 22*(1), 13–52.

Quaglia, R. J., & Lande, L. L. (2016). *Teacher voice: Amplifying success.* Thousand Oaks, CA: Corwin Press.

Rattan, A., & Ozgumus, E. (2021). Embedding mindsets in context: Theoretical considerations and opportunities for studying fixed-growth lay theories in the workplace. *Research in Organizational Behavior, 39*, Article 100127.

Ravitch, D. (2014). *Reign of error: The hoax of the privatization movement and the danger to America's public schools.* New York: Vintage.

Reflection. (n.d.). In *Merriam-Webster's online dictionary.* Accessed at www.merriam-webster.com/dictionary/reflection on December 4, 2023.

Rege, M., Hanselman, P., Solli, I. F., Dweck, C. S., Ludvigsen, S., & Bettinger, E., et al. (2021). How can we inspire nations of learners? An investigation of growth mindset and challenge-seeking in two countries. *American Psychologist, 76*(5), 755–767.

Reilly, M. A. (2008). Occasioning possibilities, not certainties: Professional learning and peer-led book clubs. *Teacher Development, 12*(3), 211–221.

Rinke, C. R. (2008). Understanding teachers' careers: Linking professional life to professional path. *Educational Research Review, 3*(1), 1–13.

Romero-Ariza, M., Quesada, A., Abril, A.-M., & Cobo, C. (2021). Changing teachers' self-efficacy, beliefs and practices through STEAM teacher professional development (Cambios en la autoeficacia, creencias y prácticas docentes en la formación STEAM de profesorado). *Journal for the Study of Education and Development, 44*(4), 942–969.

Sagor, R. (2000). *Guiding school improvement with action research.* Alexandria, VA: ASCD.

Sammons, P., Lindorff, A. M., Ortega, L., & Kington, A. (2016). Inspiring teaching: Learning from exemplary practitioners. *Journal of Professional Capital and Community, 1*(2), 124–144.

Schaefer, L., Downey, C. A., & Clandinin, D. J. (2014). Shifting from stories to live by to stories to leave by: Early career teacher attrition. *Teacher Education Quarterly, 41*(1), 9–27.

Schipper, T. M., de Vries, S., Goei, S. L., & van Veen, K. (2020). Promoting a professional school culture through lesson study? An examination of school culture, school conditions, and teacher self-efficacy. *Professional Development in Education, 46*(1), 112–129.

Schön, D. A. (1987). *Educating the reflective practitioner: Toward a new design for teaching and learning in the professions.* San Francisco: Jossey-Bass.

Scornavacco, K., Boardman, A. G., & Wang, C. (2016). Teacher leaders as change agents: Scaling up a middle school reading initiative. *Journal of School Leadership, 26*(6), 1033–1063.

See, B. H., Munthe, E., Ross, S. A., Hitt, L., & El Soufi, N. (2022). Who becomes a teacher and why? *Review of Education, 10*(3), Article e3377.

Senge, P., Cambron-McCabe, N., Lucas, T., Smith, B., Dutton, J., & Kleiner, A. (2000). *Schools that learn: A fifth discipline fieldbook for educators, parents, and everyone who cares about education.* Boston: Nicholas Brealey.

Silva, D. Y., Gimbert, B., & Nolan, J. (2000). Sliding the doors: Locking and unlocking possibilities for teacher leadership. *Teachers College Record, 102*(4), 779–804.

Simpson, J. C. (2021). Fostering teacher leadership in K-12 schools: A review of the literature. *Performance Improvement Quarterly, 34*(3), 229–246.

Sinek, S. (2011). *Start with why: How great leaders inspire everyone to take action.* New York: Portfolio/Penguin.

Sinha, S., & Hanuscin, D. L. (2017). Development of teacher leadership identity: A multiple case study. *Teaching and Teacher Education, 63*, 356–371.

Smagorinsky, P., Cook, L. S., Moore, C., Jackson, A. Y., & Fry, P. G. (2004). Tensions in learning to teach: Accommodation and the development of a teaching identity. *Journal of Teacher Education, 55*(1), 8–24.

Smeets, K., & Ponte, P. (2009). Action research and teacher leadership. *Professional Development in Education*, 35(2), 175–193.

Smith, P. S., Hayes, M. L., & Lyons, K. M. (2017). The ecology of instructional teacher leadership. *The Journal of Mathematical Behavior*, 46, 267–288.

Smith, K., & Sela, O. (2005). Action research as a bridge between pre-service teacher education and in-service professional development for students and teacher educators. *European Journal of Teacher Education*, 28(3), 293–310.

Smylie, M. A. (2010). *Continuous school improvement*. Thousand Oaks, CA: Corwin Press.

Smylie, M. A., & Denny, J. W. (1990). Teacher leadership: Tensions and ambiguities in organizational perspective. *Educational Administration Quarterly*, 26(3), 235–259.

Smylie, M. A., & Eckert, J. (2018). Beyond superheroes and advocacy: The pathway of teacher leadership development. *Educational Management Administration and Leadership*, 46(4), 556–577.

Somekh, B., & Zeichner, K. (2009). Action research for educational reform: Remodelling action research theories and practices in local contexts. *Educational Action Research*, 17(1), 5–21.

Speroni, C., Wellington, A., Burkander, P., Chiang, H., Herrmann, M., & Hallgren, K. (2020). Do educator performance incentives help students? Evidence from the teacher incentive fund national evaluation. *Journal of Labor Economics*, 38(3), 843–872.

Steele, C. F. (2009). *The inspired teacher: How to know one, grow one, or be one*. Alexandria, VA: ASCD.

Stewart, R. A., & Brendefur, J. L. (2005). Fusing lesson study and authentic achievement: A model for teacher collaboration. *Phi Delta Kappan*, 86(9), 681–687.

Stronge, J. H., Ward, T. J., & Grant, L. W. (2011). What makes good teachers good? A cross-case analysis of the connection between teacher effectiveness and student achievement. *Journal of Teacher Education*, 62(4), 339–355.

Suarez, V., & McGrath, J. (2022). *Teacher professional identity: How to develop and support it in times of change*. OECD Education Working Papers. Paris: OECD. Accessed at https://doi.org/10.1787/b19f5af7-en on February 20, 2024.

Sun, K. L. (2018). Brief report: The role of mathematics teaching in fostering student growth mindset. *Journal for Research in Mathematics Education*, 49(3), 330–335.

Tay, L. Y., Tan, L. S., Aiyoob, T. B., Tan, J. Y., Ong, M. W. L., & Ratnam-Lim, C., et al. (2023). Teacher reflection—call for a transformative mindset. *Reflective Practice: International and Multidisciplinary Perspectives*, 24(1), 27–44.

Taylor, M., Goeke, J., Klein, E., Onore, C., & Geist, K. (2011). Changing leadership: Teachers lead the way for schools that learn. *Teaching and Teacher Education*, *27*(5), 920–929.

Teacher Leadership Exploratory Consortium. (2011, February). *Teacher leader model standards*. Washington, DC: Author. Accessed at www.ets.org/content/dam/ets-org/pdfs/patl/patl-teacher-leader-model-standards.pdf on March 6, 2024.

Thompson, N., & Pascal, J. (2012). Developing critically reflective practice. *Reflective Practice: International and Multidisciplinary Perspectives*, *13*(2), 311–325.

Tsai, K. C. (2015). A preliminary meta-analysis of teacher leadership. *Journal of Education and Literature*, *3*(3), 131–137.

Tschannen-Moran, M. (2009). Fostering teacher professionalism in schools: The role of leadership orientation and trust. *Educational Administration Quarterly*, *45*(2), 217–247.

University of Illinois Urbana-Champaign. (n.d.) *Annenburg Institutes Critical Friends Summary*. Accessed at https://ws.engr.illinois.edu/sitemanager/getfile.asp?id=4190 on January 7, 2024.

Urbani, J. M., Roshandel, S., Michaels, R., & Truesdell, E. (2017). Developing and modeling 21st-century skills with preservice teachers. *Teacher Education Quarterly*, *44*(4), 27–50.

van der Heijden, H. R. M. A., Beijaard, D., Geldens, J. J. M., & Popeijus, H. L. (2018). Understanding teachers as change agents: An investigation of primary school teachers' self-perception. *Journal of Educational Change*, *19*(3), 347–373.

Van Ryzin, M. J., & Roseth, C. J. (2021). The cascading effects of reducing student stress: cooperative learning as a means to reduce emotional problems and promote academic engagement. *The Journal of Early Adolescence*, *41*(5), 700–724.

Vestad, L., & Bru, E. (2023). Teachers' support for growth mindset and its links with students' growth mindset, academic engagement, and achievements in lower secondary school. *Social Psychology of Education*.

Von Esch, K. S. (2018). Teacher leaders as agents of change: Creating contexts for instructional improvement for English learner students. *The Elementary School Journal*, *119*(1), 152–178.

Walker, D. (2013). Writing and reflection. In D. Boud, R. Keogh, & D. Walker (Eds.), *Reflection: Turning experience into learning* (pp. 52–68). New York: Routledge.

Wefald, A. J. (2022). Coaching, listening, and leadership. *Journal of Leadership Studies*. *15*(4), 58–62.

Weiner, J. M. (2011). Finding common ground: Teacher leaders and principals speak out about teacher leadership. *Journal of School Leadership*, *21*(1), 7–41.

Wenner, J. A., & Campbell, T. (2017). The theoretical and empirical basis of teacher leadership: A review of the literature. *Review of Educational Research, 87*(1), 134–171.

Wheatley, M. (2005a). *Finding our way: Leadership for an uncertain time.* San Francisco: Berrett-Koehler.

Wheatley, M. (2005b). We can be wise only together. In J. Brown, *The world café: Shaping our futures through conversations that matter* (pp. viii–xiii). San Francisco: Berrett-Koehler.

Wheatley, M. (2006a). *Leadership and the new science: Discovering order in a chaotic world* (3rd ed.). San Francisco: Berrett-Koehler.

Wheatley, M. (2006b). *Relationships: The basic building block of life.* Accessed at https://margaretwheatley.com/wp-content/uploads/2014/12/Relationships-The-Basic-Building-Blocks-of-Life.pdf on October 31, 2023.

Wiburg, K. M., & Brown, S. (2007). *Lesson study communities: Increasing achievement with diverse students.* Thousand Oaks, CA: Corwin Press.

Wilfong, R. S. (2021). The mattering model: The foundational elements of mattering for K-12 educators [Doctoral dissertation, Indiana State University] ProQuest Dissertations & Theses A&I. Accessed at https://www-proquest-com.ezproxy.indstate.edu/dissertations-theses/mattering-model-foundational-elements-k-12/docview/2537966312/se-2?accountid=11592 on March 12, 2024.

Wilfong, S., & Donlan, R. (2021, November). How mattering matters for educators. *Educational Leadership, 79*(3), 51–56.

Williams, R., & Grudnoff, L. (2011). Making sense of reflection: A comparison of beginning and experienced teachers' perceptions of reflection for practice. *Reflective Practice: International and Multidisciplinary Perspectives, 12*(3), 281–291.

Wolkenhauer, R., Hill, A. P., Dana, A. F, & Stukey, M. (2017) Exploring the connections between action research and teacher leadership: A reflection on teacher-leader research for confronting new challenges. *New Educator, 13*(2), 117–136.

Woo, H., LeTendre, G., Byun, S.-Y., & Schussler, D. (2022). Teacher leadership—collective actions, decision-making and well-being. *International Journal of Teacher Leadership, 11*(1), 29–49.

Woodcock, S., & Jones, G. (2020). Examining the interrelationship between teachers' self-efficacy and their beliefs towards inclusive education for all. *Teacher Development, 24*(4), 583–602.

Yeager, K. L., & Callahan, J. L. (2016). Learning to lead: Foundations of emerging leader identity development. *Advances in Developing Human Resources, 18*(3), 286–300.

Yeager, D. S., Carroll, J. M., Buontempo, J., Cimpian, A., Woody, S., & Crosnoe, R., et al. (2022). Teacher mindsets help explain where a growth-mindset intervention does and doesn't work. *Psychological Science*, *33*(1), 18–32.

Yeager, D. S., & Dweck, C. S. (2012). Mindsets that promote resilience: When students believe that personal characteristics can be developed. *Educational Psychologist*, *47*(4), 302–314.

York-Barr, J., & Duke, K. (2004). What do we know about teacher leadership? Findings from two decades of scholarship. *Review of Educational Research*, *74*(3), 255–316.

York-Barr, J., Sommers, W. A., Ghere, G. S., & Montie, J. (2001). *Reflective practice to improve schools: An action guide for educators*. Thousand Oaks, CA: Corwin Press.

Zemla, K., Sedek, G., Wróbel, K., Postepski, F., & Wojcik, G. M. (2023). Investigating the impact of guided imagery on stress, brain functions, and attention: A randomized trial. *Sensors*, *23*(13), Article 6210.

Zilka, A., Nussbaum, S., & Bogler, R. (2023). The relationships among growth mindset, flow, critically reflective behavior and teacher burnout. *International Journal of School and Educational Psychology*, *11*(4), 367–379.

Zulfikar, T. (2018). Understanding own teaching: Becoming reflective teachers through reflective journals. *Reflective Practice International and Multidisciplinary Perspectives*, *19*(1), 1–13.

Index

A
action research, 64–67
agency and identity, 14, 121
altruistic motivation, 7, 8.
    See also motivation
associated leadership competencies, 42
avoiding overwhelm, 96–99

B
balance, 97–99
behaviors of teachers and teacher leaders, 40
Boaler, J., 121
body awareness and muscle relaxation, 107
book clubs
    professional learning and, 62–63
    reproducibles for, 70–71
breathing/deep breathing, 107
Brown, B., 85
building and sustaining healthy relationships.
    See relationships

C
Caniëls, M., 126
Cashman, K., 30
catalysts for change, 49
change through collaboration
    about, 51–53
    collaboration, 56–59
    collective teacher efficacy and, 55–56
    conclusion, 69
    professional learning and, 60–69
    reflective practice and dialogue and, 59–60
    reproducibles for, 70–78
    self-efficacy and, 54–55
classroom supporters, 49. *See also* teachers and teacher leaders
classroom teachers, 32. *See also* teachers and teacher leaders
coaches. *See also* teachers and teacher leaders
    data coaches, 49
    supporting resilience and, 102
    teacher leader competencies and, 42
    teacher leader growth and, 33
cognitive empathy, 85
collaboration. *See also* change through collaboration
    about, 56–59
    relationships and, 80
collaborative inquiry, 56, 63, 64, 72
collaborative teams, 68–69
collective teacher efficacy, 55–56.
    See also efficacy
collegiality, 58, 80
communication, 92–93
compassion, 101
competencies, teacher leader competencies, 41–42
confidence, 55
congeniality, 58
continual reflection for growth, 37
critical friends, 66. *See also* relationships

cultivating a growth mindset. *See* growth mindsets
curiosity and growth mindsets, 131
curriculum specialists, 48. *See also* teachers and teacher leaders

D

Danielson, C., 31
data coaches, 49. *See also* coaches
domains, 43, 44. *See also* standards, teacher leader model standards
Duke, K., 31
Dweck, C., 119–120

E

effecting change through collaboration. *See* change through collaboration
efficacy
    classroom supporters and, 49
    collective teacher efficacy, 55–56
    self-efficacy, 54–55
    teacher leadership efficacy, 44
emotional intelligence. *See also* relationships
    about, 83–85
    communication and, 92–93
    honoring others' voices and, 92
    listening and, 85–87
    presence, being present, 90–91
    respect and, 88, 90
    time, spending together, 87–88
    trust and, 91
empathy, 84, 85
extrinsic motivation, 7, 8, 9. *See also* motivation

F

fixed mindsets, understanding growth and fixed mindsets, 119–129. *See also* growth mindsets
focusing on your purpose
    about, 5–6
    acting, keeping it real, and revisiting, 24–25
    conclusion, 25
    creating your purpose story, 20–24
    knowing why you teach, 6–9
    reflecting on your purpose, 9–17
formal roles, 31

foundational competencies, 41
Fullan, M., 56
function approaches to teacher leadership, 31. *See also* teachers and teacher leaders

G

glows and grows, 125
goals and resilience, 100
gratitude and optimism, 132
grit and growth mindsets, 132–133
growing as a teacher and leader. *See also* teachers and teacher leaders
    about, 27–30
    conclusion, 50
    leadership in teaching careers, 47–50
    teacher leader growth, 32–33, 36–38
    teacher leadership, 30–32
    teacher leadership skills, 38–47
growth mindsets. *See also* mindsets
    about, 117, 119
    conclusion, 133
    developing a growth mindset, 129–133
    understanding growth and fixed mindsets, 119–129
guided imagery, 107

H

Hattie, J., 55, 59
honoring others' voices, 92
Hunzicker, J., 65
hybrid teacher leaders, 32. *See also* teachers and teacher leaders

I

informal roles, 31
instructional competencies, 42
instructional specialists, 48. *See also* teachers and teacher leaders
intrinsic motivation, 7, 8, 9. *See also* motivation
introduction
    about teachers and leadership, 1–2
    about this book, 3–4
    who this book is for, 4

J

Jacobs, R., 10

L

Law of Influence, 30
leadership compass, 37
leadership in teaching careers, 47–50. *See also* teachers and teacher leaders
lesson studies, 67–68
listening
    developing a growth mindset and, 130–131
    emotional intelligence and, 85–87

M

Margolis, J., 31
mastery experiences, 54
McEachen, J., 56
meaning systems, 119
mentors. *See also* teachers and teacher leaders
    formal roles and, 48
    hybrid teacher leaders and, 32
    professional learning and, 64
    supporting resilience and, 102
    teacher leader competencies and, 42
    teacher leader growth and, 33
mindfulness and meditation, 101, 106
mindsets. *See also* growth mindsets
    meaning systems and, 119
    teacher mindsets about leadership, 126–129
    teacher mindsets about student learning, 121–122, 124
    teacher mindsets about teaching, 124–126
motivation
    emotional intelligence and, 84
    knowing why you teach, 7–9
    reflecting on your purpose, 10

O

ongoing professional learning, 37–38
overarching competencies, 41–42

P

personal interpretive frameworks, 13
physical exercise, 106
policy competencies, 42
positional teacher leadership, 47. *See also* teachers and teacher leaders

presence, being present, 90–91
professional learning
    about, 60–62
    action research and, 64–67
    book clubs and, 62–63
    collaborative teams and, 68–69
    lesson studies and, 67–68
    mentoring and, 64
    ongoing professional learning, 37–38
purpose stories, 20–25. *See also* focusing on your purpose

Q

Quinn, J., 56

R

Ravitch, D., 8
reflecting on your purpose. *See also* focusing on your purpose
    about, 9–11
    future, 17
    past, 11–14
    present, 14, 16–17
reflection
    continual reflection for growth, 37
    developing a growth mindset and, 131
    reflective practice and dialogue, 59–60
    self-knowledge and, 83
Reign of Error: The Hoax of the Privatization Movement and the Danger to America's Public Schools (Ravitch), 8
relationships
    about, 79–81
    conclusion, 93
    emotional intelligence and, 83–93
    reproducibles for, 94
    self-knowledge and, 81–83
    supporting resilience and, 102
Renders, I., 126
reproducibles for
    action plan for wellness worksheet, 109–112
    collegial conversations: a process for reflection, dialogue, and feedback with peers, 74
    my ongoing journey as an agent of change, 75–78
    nuts and bolts of book clubs, 70–71

reflecting on my reactions, 94
reflections for collaborative inquiry,
    72–73
wellness check-in, 113–115
resilience
    avoiding overwhelm, 96
    supporting, 100–103
resources providers, 49
respect, 88, 90
roles
    formal and informal leadership roles,
        31–32
    leadership in teaching careers, 47–50
    relationships and, 80–81

S

salaries, 9
school culture, 103
school leaders, 49. *See also* teachers and
    teacher leaders
self-awareness, 56, 84, 88
self-care
    about, 95
    avoiding overwhelm and, 96–99
    conclusion, 108
    reducing stress and, 105–108
    reproducibles for, 109–115
    supporting resilience and, 100–103
self-efficacy, 54–55. *See also* efficacy
self-esteem, 102–103
self-knowledge, 81–83
self-regulation, 84, 88, 91
Semeijn, J., 126
semi-formal roles, 31
Sinek, S., 10, 11
social persuasion, 54
social skills, 85. *See also* emotional
    intelligence
socialization influences, 8
split, 11
standards, teacher leader model standards,
    43–45

stress
    avoiding overwhelm, 96
    reducing stress, 105–108

T

taking care of yourself. *See* self-care
teacher leadership skills
    growing as a teacher and leader, 38–47
    teacher leader competencies, 41–42
    teacher leader model standards, 43–45
teachers and teacher leaders
    definition of teacher leadership, 31
    growing as a teacher and leader, 30–32
    leadership in teaching careers, 47–50
    teacher and teacher leader
        behaviors, 40
    teacher leadership efficacy, 44
    teacher mindsets about leadership,
        126–129
    teacher mindsets about student
        learning, 121–122, 124
    teacher mindsets about teaching,
        124–126
time
    avoiding overwhelm, 97
    emotional intelligence and, 87–88
trust, 91

V

verbal persuasion, 54–55
vicarious experiences, 54
voices, honoring others,' 92

W

Wheatley, M., 79, 86
why, your, 10, 11. *See also* focusing on
    your purpose
workload, 99

Y

York-Barr, J., 31

200+ Proven Strategies for Teaching Reading, Grades K–8
Kathy Perez

This easy-to-use reference guide provides K–8 teachers with practical strategies to motivate all students to develop their reading abilities across grade levels and content areas and to help students who are struggling with reading make great strides in literacy achievement.
BKF663

Teacher Leaders, Classroom Champions
Jeanetta Jones Miller

Gain a clear path to activate school improvement from within your classroom. This book shares a vision of teacher leadership not as teachers who lead other teachers but as those who take responsibility in supporting other teachers, students, and families in a variety of ways.
BKG110

Training Teacher Leaders in a PLC at Work®
Jasmine K. Kullar

In this book, author Jasmine K. Kullar empowers teacher leadership teams with the knowledge to implement the PLC process successfully while developing ten essential leadership skills that will help influence their colleagues to advance student achievement.
BKG201

Leadership at Every Level
Janelle Clevenger McLaughlin

Nurture your leadership skills and grow as a lifelong learner with the support of *Leadership at Every Level*. Ideal for book studies, this resource shares practical, research-based strategies for strengthening leadership capacity at the classroom, school, and district levels.
BKG014

Solution Tree | Press

Visit SolutionTree.com or call 800.733.6786 to order.

Live your best life

ON-SITE AND VIRTUAL PROFESSIONAL LEARNING

Discover **practical, research-affirmed daily routines and strategies** you can use to avoid prolonged stress, physical and emotional exhaustion, and burnout. The benefit? Educators who feel supported and fulfilled in their work will bring their best selves each day to support student success.

Partner with our Wellness Solutions for Educators™ experts to:

- Understand how educator wellness leads to improved student achievement
- Discover a framework for enhancing the health and well-being of all educators
- Explore four core dimensions of professional wellness

> *Live your best life! We took time today to focus on educator wellness. When we are at our best, our students get the best! It was an absolutely amazing day.*
>
> —Dr. Megan Baker, principal, Magnolia Parkway Elementary, Texas

Learn more
888.763.9045
SolutionTree.com/WellnessMatters